WANDERLUST

BOOK DISCUSSION AND SIGNING
PLUS SPECIAL GUESTS!

CACTUS MUSIC!
SATURDAY OCT. 26, 1 PM
Beverages Provided By St. Arnold Brewing Co
2110 Portsmouth St, Houston, TX 77098

ZIA RECORDS
PRESENTS
"TOXIC SHOCK RECORDS" BILL SASSENBERGER BOOK SIGNING

ZIA RECORDS (THUNDERBIRD, PHOENIX)
TUESDAY, JULY 9
2-4PM

ZIA RECORDS (SPEEDWAY, TUCSON)
SATURDAY, JULY 13
2-4PM

TOXIC SHOCK CHRONICLES THE HISTORY OF THE PUNK RECORD STORE/MAIL ORDER ENTERPRISE/RECORD LABEL FROM ITS ORIGINS IN 1980 IN THE GRIMY SUBURBS OF POMONA, CA TO ITS DEMISE IN TUCSON, AZ IN 2014.

Book Signing
with the man who brought us Toxic Shock Records
Bill Sassenberger

Sun. July 21st 2024
From 1:00 pm to 3:00 pm
Singles Going Steady
2219 Second Ave. Sea. Wa. 98121
(206) 441-7396

BILL SASSENBERGER

WANDERLUST AND WELCOME MATS

"The Broccoli Chronicles"

The Sequel to Toxic Shock Records - Assassin of Mediocrity

© Bill Sassenberger, 2026

www.ToxicShockRecords.com
azhwy666@yahoo.com

ISBN: 979-8-234-01971-4 (paperback)
Library of Congress Control Number: 2026908408

Interior layout and design by Welly Artcore: artcorefanzine@gmail.com
Cover art by Brian Walsby. Back cover photo by Amanda MacKaye.
Back cover artwork by Vincent "Ransid" Packard. All other photos by
either Sara Stover or Bill Sassenberger unless otherwise noted.

10 9 8 7 6 5 4 3 2 1

Published by Toxic Shock Publishing
PO Box 2091 Tucson AZ 85702, U.S.A.

Printed in the U.S.A.

CONTENTS

Stump Pass FL (photo by Paula Ramsey)
Outside Tonopah AZ
Bay Bridge San Francisco CA

the Spit Homer AK
PIER
ONE
THEATRE
BE NICE
OR
Leave!
WELCOME!

Oceanside 2019 - Julianna's memorial with:
Adrian (Front) Mindi, Sue, Dan, Diane, Me, Paul and Adam (Rear L-R)
Bisbee, AZ
Petrified Forest, AZ

Part One – Lost and Found

When my wife Julianna passed away on March 27th, 2019, I was left alone, living in an empty house. Her two sisters, Adrian and Mindi, had stayed with me for a few days after her death, helping with such emotional tasks as making arrangements for the cremation. After taking some of her belongings for themselves, they tried to lighten my load by helping me sell the abundance of Julianna's trinkets and clothes. For years, she enjoyed collecting costume jewelry and kaftans and such, mostly on eBay. There was just so much of it! It was disheartening to find out that items that gave her so much joy, that she had treasured so much, had very little real value on the resale market. In the end, they were just a massive pile of things. Without the person, these were just mere objects. It was the person who gave them value.

For spiritual fortitude, they went with me into Zia Records to pick up the brand new Meat Puppets album, Dusty Notes—a CD to play in the car and the vinyl LP for home. For several years now, Julianna and I had looked forward to attending their annual post-Thanksgiving shows at the Crescent ballroom in Phoenix. Always a good time. When I brought my purchases to the counter, the clerk handed me a flyer for an in-store performance the Pups were doing the following week up in Tempe. Julianna and I had listened to their single Nine Pins online just days before she was hospitalized. Now, three weeks later, she was gone.

I called up my friend Matt Thompson in Phoenix to see if he wanted to go with me, since he was the only one I really knew up there and I didn't feel like going alone. We hung out by the merch table and Matt introduced me to Linda Kite, their long-time friend and swag slinger. As the widow of D. Boon, the guitarist and singer from the influential San Pedro band the Minutemen, Linda had a long history with the band members of the Meat Puppets. The two bands had toured together many times in the 1980s and had developed a strong kinship over that time period. On December 22, 1985 Linda was behind the wheel with her fiance asleep in the back when the vans rear axle broke and D. Boon was ejected and tragically lost his life. They were headed towards Santa Fe on vacation and planned on stopping in Phoenix to rest at the Kirkwood brothers house. At Zia, the band played a great short set, including a number of songs from the new album. After the set, they were signing posters and records, so I got in line with all the Meat Puppets vinyl I had brought with me. I've never been much of a fanboy, so this was a first. When I awkwardly tried to explain to them how much their music—over several decades—had meant to me and my recently deceased wife, they were very gracious and kind. Curt told me to "Hang in there," which I took to heart. I was getting a little too choked up to stay much longer, so I took my stash of autographed music and hit the road back to Tucson.

I never thought of myself as ever becoming a homeowner. Since leaving high school, I had always been a renter. I had always thought home ownership was beyond my reach. I had lousy credit and no money saved up. Everywhere we lived, we rented, whether it was Pomona, New Orleans, Bisbee or Tucson. However, we lucked into a unique situation where the house we rented in the Armory Park neighborhood became for sale. In 1993, the home's owner, former priest and suspected pedophile Claude Prince, offered us an option to take over his mortgage payments. The offer came with the condition that we give him a sizable down payment on the home loan. We borrowed money from some credit cards and Julianna's student loan to make it possible. It took a few difficult years before his share was paid off and then we took over the actual mortgage.

The house was in a historic neighborhood that had seen better days. Armory Park was the first primarily Caucasian neighborhood built for railroad workers when the railway first came to town at the turn of the century. Its epicenter was an actual U.S. Army barracks built for the soldiers to protect early Tucson settlers from Apache raids. Now it's surrounded by mostly red brick houses. The streets are extra wide, which I recently found out were designed to allow horse-drawn carriages to make U-turns. Architecture styles, Territorial, Victorian (with their distinctive witches hat towers) and Craftsman,imported from east of the Mississippi, dominated the neighborhood, a distinct alternative to the mud brick adobes in the original sleepy barrios.

Before the railroad came to town, Tucson was sparsely inhabited. Its population would explode once air conditioning was invented, but that was decades yet to come. Double brick, like adobe, would insulate against the summer heat and open-air back porches (Arizona rooms) would be for sleeping on hot summer nights.

Some of these new houses were nicer than others, as there were obvious class differences. White collar employees, the engineers, and conductors got the nicer, more elaborate Victorian spreads and the grunts who actually built the damn railroad, Eastern Europeans and the Chinese, got the more basic accommodations like boarding houses, duplexes and shotgun shacks. On many of the street corners, there were grocery stores run by Chinese immigrants, who sold fresh produce and other staples of frontier life. They also served as money lenders. Many early Tucsonans like the Buffalo Soldiers and Mexicans didn't trust the banks, but were willing to allow the Chinese merchants to hang on to their money and the merchants on the corner would, in turn, make small loans to members of the community. We had one of the bigger Chinese corner shops, the OK Market, next door to us, but by the '90s it was just another abandoned structure, home to many disgruntled pigeons and feral cats.

Our house was built in 1916—at least the original first level was. A large porch in the front, the inside had the original wood floors that were sadly, atrociously painted white. There were some Craftsman-style built-in bookshelves, glass china cabinets and a corner desk. The kitchen also had the original wood cabinets, ice box and concrete sink, which was cracked and butt ugly. When doing some repairs in the crawlspace, a plumber found a wood handled ice pick from a local company that used to deliver blocks of ice to the neighborhood.

Sometime in the '80s, the priest (or his predecessor) installed a wrought iron spiral staircase in the back of the house, bricked in the Arizona room and built an upper level with two small bed rooms. There was also a wooden balcony that looked out over a neighbor's parking lot and Tucson's southside. A couple steps above these rooms led to a larger loft space/attic made into a bedroom tucked under the roof, with an unfinished bathroom and a slanted, low ceiling. Underneath the balcony, a redwood deck was built, wrapping around the back of the house to the rear entrance. A sunken jacuzzi with an insulated cover was installed in 1980.

The neighboring area was checkered with a few houses fallen into neglect and since the downtown Greyhound Bus station was within a few blocks, we got our share of foot traffic from transients. We were burglarized a few times over the early years and a couple of times the culprits were actually caught in the act and arrested. One was a serial/cereal burglar, who would always eat the breakfast cereal in the home before leaving the scene of the crime. Crack cocaine addiction, not sugar, was the real reason behind the flurry of break-ins in the neighborhood.

We spent years gradually making improvements to the house. After installing security bars in all our windows to deter break ins, the first home improvement project was laying tile over the kitchen countertop.

Then upstairs, we installed a toilet, a sink in the bathroom and tiled the shower stall. Much later, we got lucky when a matching money grant from the city we applied for was approved in 2008, so we took out a home equity loan to get a new roof, replace the wonky chain link fencing, upgrade some drafty windows and install linoleum, tile, and wood flooring for the living room.

Fast forward to April 2019 when Julianna's sisters had left town and I was now truly alone. In the past eight years, I had lost my mom, two sisters and two brothers, but my wife's passing struck me the hardest. The record store that we had founded had been closed for five years but I was still working. As I had been since 2012, I was a home-based airline reservation agent, working a five-hour shift in one of the upstairs rooms I had converted into an office. I was also selling leftover stock from Toxic Ranch online and made runs to the post office several times a week. I considered this my punk rock pension.

When I got off my corporate lackey shift, the stark emptiness of the house really hit me. After spending decades inseparable from my wife, I dreaded getting off work, as that kept my mind occupied. The night time was the worst. I joined an online widowers support group, but it was mostly too depressing to read the posts and I really didn't feel like sharing my own personal experience. I put the word out on a Facebook post to see if any of my friends or acquaintances knew of anyone looking to rent a room. I was hoping to find a tenant from a group of folks that I kind of knew, as opposed to a total stranger that I might find on Craigslist. I wanted to bring some life into this empty space to ward off the feeling of isolation.

I had heard of Airbnb, how it had ruined urban neighborhoods across the country, including our beloved New Orleans, and that it made rentals harder to find and rent prices to increase. I had never used it myself, because for the last seven years as a caregiver, I hadn't been doing much traveling. We had stayed in a couple of bed and breakfast places, but that was over twenty years ago.

About five years earlier, I started a project to convert a dilapidated brick structure next to the house (just a shed actually, once a horse stable with a dirt floor) into a wheelchair-friendly casita with an adjacent new bathroom designed for easier showers, one where a shower chair would easily fit. It was a real burden to give Julianna a shower or even to use the toilet in the master bathroom in the old house. We both dreaded it, the space was just so tight.

The long-term plan had been to rent out the house and live in the casita. It would make our "golden years" easier. The rental income would supplement our retirement. The casita would be roomy enough to navigate Julianna's wheelchair into the new bathroom with ample space. A floating sink would allow her to use that much more easily too, a, much needed improvement to our "quality of life," as they say, whoever "they" are.

We had to lay new brick for the collapsed walls, construct a roof, pour concrete for the floor, install plumbing, and dig a new sewer line for the bathroom. The last task was a mammoth undertaking—digging a 100-foot trench three feet deep through dirt, rocks and a hardened layer of mineral deposits called caliche to the main line.

The whole project was worked on in stages, as I could afford it, over a five year period with the bulk done by a local musician and master carpenter, Lucas Moseley and the connections he had made with plumbing-and concrete workers.. By early 2019, all was complete except for some finishing touches like electricity, doors and windows. The other missing link was Julianna. She wasn't there to share it with me.

In April 2019, we had a memorial service for her out in Oceanside, one of our favorite places to visit in recent years. Her two sisters and brother attended, along with my cousin Sue, who lived in Oceanside, as well as my brother's widow Diane and her two sons. I spread some of her ashes in the marina there. I'm glad they were all there to support me, for it was a very sobering day. Before we spread her ashes, to lighten the somber mood, Julianna's sister Mindi recalled how she marveled at her sister mooning passing cars on the 4th of July while waving an American flag. That image got us a good laugh, which we all needed.

Another trip I had planned before Julianna passed, was to revisit Spokane. I saw that Neil Young was doing a series of solo shows in the Northwest and one was at the Fox Theatre in Spokane. I had asked Julianna if she wanted to go, but she didn't seem too keen on the idea. To my surprise, she actually suggested I take Ann Marie instead, my estranged birth daughter whom I hadn't seen in person since a family reunion back in 1995 at the North Rim of the Grand Canyon.

Not long after Ann Marie got out of high school, I took my mom up to Oregon to try and reconnect after an eighteen-year gap. It was an odd and bittersweet experience, especially finding out that her adoptive parents were deeply entrenched in the Pentecostal movement. We attended a church service, where I was surprised to witness several worshippers "talking in tongues", which seemed like totally absurd gibberish to me. I held my opinion to myself and just smiled.

A few years later, I attended her wedding with my brother Ron, which became awkward when I introduced myself as her father to some people I didn't know in her small town of Newberg. Her soon-to-be husband took great offense at these words, stating I was never there when it counted, and that I had some nerve claiming to be her father. My last in-person visit with her was when her daughter Morgan was a newborn. After that, I stayed in touch with her through occasional letters, e-mails and Christmas cards. Eventually Facebook replaced all those but unfortunately I can't honestly say we ever became all that close.

Now it is May, 2019. I decided to grab a ticket to the Spokane concert and took a couple days off from work to fly up and check it out. It made perfect sense to me to go alone. Neil Young was playing solo without any backing musicians and here I was again, also solo, after many years of marriage with the last seven and a half years spent as a full- time caregiver. I needed to rediscover who I was as a person, not unlike when I moved to Spokane when I was eighteen in 1973, except now I had decades of life experience under my belt.

When I rented a car at the airport, I was advised that the city had just experienced a major flood and to drive carefully. Got myself a french dip sandwich at Longhorn BBQ and some sleep at a nondescript hotel in an unfamiliar area of town and in the morning drove downtown to see what I could recognize. I heard on the news that the theater Neil was playing in had some partial flood damage, but the concert was still on. I walked around the amazing red brick architecture of historic downtown, past the Hotel Carlyle, a derelict hotel that was one of the most dilapidated places I'd ever lived in. Definitely creepy. They say it's filled with ghosts. Not sure about all that but I do remember I got crabs here from an old couch. It was still being used for very low-income housing and had kept that dark and haunted vibe, even in the bright summer daylight.

I walked over the bridge by the Spokane River Falls, to discover the Black Angus steakhouse where I had once washed dishes as a recently incarcerated teenager on a work release program was now a seafood restaurant overlooking the river. The World's Fair of 1974 had some structures still intact and was now a public park.

Having all day to kill time, I took in a movie, one of those John Wick flicks with over-the-top violence and loud jarring sounds. "People find this entertaining?", I thought to myself. After poking around a small record store, I bought a marijuana rollie at a dispensary and while walking down the sidewalk smoking it, realized I was being followed by two cops. This might have terrified me in 1974 but today that paranoia was ancient history due to legalisation. These cops were just doing crowd control duty for the annual Lilac Festival parade that was taking place on the streets of downtown.

After walking around all day, it became apparent that my new shoes were too tight and I was looking forward to tonight's concert with assigned seats. I admired the Silver Eagle, the vintage chrome bus that Neil travels in, that was sitting idly in the parking lot. I got in line to enter the Fox theatre and found my seat in the restored 1931 art deco movie palace. A friendly couple sat next to me and started chatting me up. The wife said she knew nothing about Neil Young's music other than a couple of the big hits like Heart of Gold and Harvest Moon. I mentioned I was more into the Ditch Trilogy albums and she looked at me with a confused look. She had to point out to me that her hubby was growing a beard and wasn't planning to shave it off until he shot his first buck of the season. He just smiled at me broadly and I was quite relieved when the music finally started.

It seemed like Neil was just improvising his set list, picking out songs as he went along, indiscriminately choosing which instrument to pick up, from one guitar to another, then piano to pump organ. Neil told the crowd that tonight's show was sponsored by water, a nod to his anti-corporate jingle, This Note's for You. At one point, as he fumbled along mid-set changing guitars, a heckler yelled out "You're confused", maybe as a way to protest Neil's progressive politics. Evidently, the friendly, hippie population of 1970's Spokane was now partly inhabited by the Fox News crowd by 2019. Regardless, it was an excellent twenty one song set ending with Tumbleweed on ukulele. My new friend got her two favorite songs and I got to hear The Losing End and a loud electric version of Ohio.

Back at home, on June 2nd, I drove up to the Petrified Forest, another of Julianna's favorite places back in her pre-stroke life. With a heavy heart, I spread more of her ashes there in a spot overlooking the Painted Desert. I remembered it was one of her requests that she mentioned to me once in the 80's and I wanted to honor her wishes. It was a sad, lonely trip, driving up from Tucson, stopping at a rest stop by the Salt River, near Apache Falls.

In Show Low, I had an overnight visit with my niece Lori and her husband, an amusing character who was the human spitting image of Boomhauer from the cartoon King of the Hill. I hadn't seen them since 2011 when they visited me briefly at Toxic Ranch Records. Her mom, my sister Curl, had recently passed away from COPD and like me, was dealing with the effects of grief.. They lived outside of town in a two-story log cabin and invited me to spend the night. She was working as a public defender and was looking forward to a new position representing clients at Fort Apache. I shared the details of how Julianna had died from a nasty internal infection that quickly led to sepsis, telling how terribly difficult it was for me to come to the realization that she wasn't going to recover from it and how hard it was to let her go.

Later that month I went out to the Essence of Tranquility, a low-brow mineral hot springs spa just outside of Safford, about two hours from Tucson. It was an off-the-beaten path place that my friend Lucas Mosely had recommended a couple of years ago. It was relaxing to soak in the concrete pools of warm water and the spa was in a very rustic and funky setting. Each pool had a different theme, such as Roman, heart shaped, and tropical. They also offered hippie shacks made of storage sheds and other simple structures where you could spend the night, which I did. They had a huge VHS library next to the communal kitchen. I listened to the whimsical, yet melancholy songs from a Fats Waller CD on the drive there and back and thought how I might incorporate some of this same laid-back ambiance at home.

In July, I was offered a cat-sitting opportunity in Berkeley, from Deanna Ewers, the twin sister of a former employee in Pomona who had heard of my new widower status. That was a completely unexpected gesture and it was certainly a welcome respite from the summer heat of Tucson. In a nice residential neighborhood of vintage houses, I had a free place to stay in exchange for the simple obligation of pampering her adorable cats. How could I refuse?

I also got to hang out with her brother David Ewers for a day, who took me out to Joaquin Miller Park, which sits on a hill overlooking the Oakland area. David was the last employee we had in Pomona, who kept Toxic Shock open there while we settled down in Tucson. It was great seeing him again. He showed me the Moses pyramid made of rocks. It's just up the hill from a small, battered white cabin. Nearby, a stone funeral pyre collects eucalyptus leaves by a bench with one of the best views in the Bay Area. From this lookout point, you get a spectacular view of the bay bridge and you could see the cargo ships from China approaching the harbor. These crude obscurities were all built by one eccentric man over a century ago — a poet, adventurer, scoundrel and celebrity of his time who went by the name of Joaquin Miller. Before he built his strange empire in Oakland, Miller lived an extraordinary life with many bizarre adventures. As a child Miller moved to Oregon and then made his way to California during the Gold Rush. There, he was involved in numerous battles with Native Americans. After getting struck in the cheek with an arrow in one conflict, Miller claims he sided with the Native Americans and was run out of town. It's written that after battle Miller did indeed live alongside the Wintu tribe in Northern California, and even fathered a daughter, Cali-Shasta, also known as Lily of the Shasta, with a Native woman. In 1859, Miller was arrested and jailed for stealing a horse in Shasta County, where he claims he was broken out of jail by his bride. In Idaho in the 1860s, Miller was elected as a judge in Grant County. In Alaska he lost two toes to frostbite. In

New York he married a third wife. Between working as cook, a judge, a newspaper editor, Pony Express rider and poet, Miller also found the time to join mercenary William Walker on his invasion of Nicaragua, where Miller's friend somehow became dictator.

That summer, I was asked by Mikey Bean to contribute some words to an oral history book called Phantoms: The Rise of Deathrock from the LA Punk Scene. It had a feature on Rozz Williams and early Christian Death and he wanted my input, with a focus on the Pomona Toxic Shock connection. This may have been another trigger to write a book of my own. Looking back on those days inspired me to document my experiences prior to this time and after and I made a note to myself to get started on that and to make it more than just a passing thought.

At this point in my life, I had decided instead of living in my own ghost world, it was important for me to reconnect with more friends and family I hadn't seen in many years. I started with my bookish friend Peter in Vallejo whom I've known since 1979 when he was working at Systematic Distribution and later at Last Gasp. I also paid another visit to my cousin Sue in Oceanside (who was a great help in organizing the memorial), and my only surviving sibling, my sister Mary (who I've always called Mimi) in Camarillo. I also visited her daughter, my niece Debbie, who had moved from California to New Orleans in 1987. Even after Katrina, she decided to stay in the city. I wanted to see the World War Two Museum, which was a new impressive addition to New Orleans. Overall, that was a very sentimental trip, seeing our favorite city for the first time in thirty years, and returning to Tucson by rail on the Sunset Limited, at Amtrak's leisurely pace.

I started to look into this Airbnb concept and a site called Vrbo. It was surprisingly simple to get started. I took several photos of the rooms in the house and uploaded them from my cell phone. I added descriptions, highlighting the quiet neighborhood and its close proximity to the now bustling and increasingly gentrified downtown. At first, I tried to list the entire house with its four bedrooms and two bathrooms, figuring it would appeal to a traveling family on vacation. I priced it comparatively to other listings on the site. Nothing happened. I lowered the price, bit by bit, and still crickets. I was talking to my friend Bruno—who came over sporadically to print t-shirts—and told him what I was doing. He told me to try renting out just the rooms, not the entire house.

This turned out to be a game changer. My first Airbnb booking came in—a party of two for the master bed room downstairs. A photo of the guest and his hometown popped up on the app, a guy named Mustang. I cleaned up the house.and got the room ready. I had moved most of my personal stuff into the casita and started sleeping there. The check-in day approached and I wasn't sure what to expect. It was certainly a new experience having strangers using my house as their temporary lodging.

I assumed it was going to be a man and wife on holiday. As the night wore on, they finally pulled up and I went out to greet them. This became a habit of mine. If someone was staying in my house, at the bare minimum, I'd at least like to meet them. Some guests seemed to find that odd, as they preferred total anonymity with keycodes and lockboxes.

Mustang smelled of smoke and body odor and so did his male buddy. It turned out they were firefighters, taking a break from their job in Flagstaff. Mustang looked at the queen mattress puzzledly and asked if there was another bed for his partner. I thought for a second and remembered I had a room upstairs that was more or less ready. During their short stay, they drank a couple of cases of beer and made a big pot full of spaghetti. They emptied the trash and cleaned up after themselves before they checked out, so it was fine.

quin Miller Park, Oakland, CA 2019 with David Ewers
Essence of Tranquility, outside Safford, AZ
13B
4B
New Orleans, Graveyard
Union Station, Los Angeles

My next booking was from a guy from Malaysia. I thought, "Okay, this might be interesting." I might learn some things from a different culture. It turned out he was a student at ASU and drove down to Tucson expressly to have sex with his girlfriend who was going to the U of A. He told me he wanted to visit Tucson on a regular basis and wanted to get my phone number to make arrangements with me directly and pay in cash.

He was a tad protective of me interacting with his girlfriend. She was friendly, but he would stand awkwardly between us, acting defensively as we made small talk. He left me a good review, yet complained about the dim street lighting, something I had no control over. I never heard from him again. I'm thinking they probably broke up, but who knows?

I got a booking from Twentynine Palms for two people, with a note stating they were visiting town to attend a wedding. When I met them, it was obvious they were Marines from the base there. I told them I spent my teenage years in the same town and couldn't wait to get the hell out of there. That was about all we had in common.

They were kind of loud and slightly obnoxious. They were hanging out by the outdoor jacuzzi after midnight and I heard one say to the other, "Let's go back and get that girl at the Waffle House." Sure enough, an hour or so later, they brought her back to continue their little splash party until way past 3:00 a.m.

I did get a couple of responses from my Facebook post. In July, a newspaper photographer acquaintance knew of another photojournalist, Josh from Wyoming, who was looking for lodging on his temporary assignment for the Arizona Daily Star newspaper. Josh was easy-going and interesting to chat with. We talked about punk rock and how even Wyoming had a small scene. I told him I was kicking around the idea of putting my life story into a book, with an emphasis on how punk changed the trajectory of my life. He rented the upstairs loft for a couple of months. When I returned from my September trip to New Orleans, he let me know he was moving on.

Matt Brown, a customer of the record store from the early '90s, shared the room rental info with his mother in Seattle, who was considering a move to Tucson. She got in touch and came down for a week to check out the city. Janet was very nice, quick-witted, a little older than I, and had quite the life experience. Born in New York City, she grew up in rural Alaska and settled in Seattle, where she raised two sons. She then spent eight years in Thailand as a single woman over the age of fifty. Not only a voracious reader, Janet was also an author, writing and publishing three books about her experiences. She liked the bigger space upstairs and also the neighborhood so she handed me a cash deposit for a six-month stay and arrived in October with a small suitcase and her cat.

Fiercely independent, Janet loved roaming the streets of Tucson on foot and by bus. As part of my daily routine, I would put the daily newspaper under her door when I had finished reading it. We would converse about current events, mostly about Trump's latest idiotic nonsense. My two cats, Mr Peanut and Harry, enjoyed invading her room while her cat Mulrooney cowered in fear. Their feline hijinks never failed to keep us amused and entertained.

Meanwhile, the other short-term guests came and went. We had a lovely visitor from France, who arrived by train with her twelve-year-old son, and a few friendly tourists from China, Spain, Germany and Denmark. They all seemed to enjoy the cats, the laid-back ambiance, and the poster art (leftovers from the record store) that I used to decorate the walls.

In November, I tapped into some unused vacation time. I went up to catch the Meat Puppets once again, when they played their annual post-Thanksgiving show, then drove out to Yucca Valley to meet up with my nephews Dan and Darren DelCastillo from L.A. to catch the band again at Pappy and Harriet's in Pioneertown, near Yucca Valley. Both shows were life-affirmingly great. We spent the night at the Joshua Tree Inn, where in 1973, Gram Parsons had overdosed in one of their rooms. I drove back to Phoenix and spent a night at my friend Matt's house, where I got my ass kicked at chess by his son, Jesse. From there, I flew standby from Sky Harbor, trying to make my way to Amsterdam. I had renewed my passport and wanted to take more advantage of my employee benefits of free travel. Now, more than ever, I realized life is a fleeting experience and I yearned to see more of the world.

I caught a plane to Charlotte, then to Frankfurt, and from there took a high-speed train to Holland. In Amsterdam I had my first experience as an Airbnb guest, staying in a garden shack next to a houseboat on the river. It was rainy and very cold outside, but the shack was kept cozy with a furnace that used wood pellets for heat. My hosts rented me a bike without hand brakes, so when it wasn't raining, I took that into the city. With millions of other bikes easily passing me by, I took a canal tour and visited the Van Gogh Museum.

Daniel House and his wife Patty came to Tucson for a quick visit in December. It was nice to catch up with another old friend from the music biz and he interviewed me for a Skin Yard book that he had been working on. I thought to myself, "Is everyone I know writing a book? What's my excuse?"

Christmas of 2019 was a particularly rough one emotionally, being the first time in thirty-eight years that I spent the holiday without Julianna. In January, we had a peculiar guest. I was getting third-party bookings now, where people on the site would book a room for other people. This one was from a lady with a Chinese last name, but the guest was a guy named Juan from Mexico. He was nice and polite, claiming to be a Bible salesman or something. He had a very heavy duffel with him and as he lugged it up and down the spiral staircase, we couldn't help but notice the clanking sound. Janet and I suspected it might be guns not Bibles inside the duffel. Regardless, I ended up with another positive review.

My next guest was a guy named Reswan from Bangladesh (via Colorado) who, after he had settled in, changed out of his western attire into his traditional sarong called a lungi. We had some meaningful conversations about life during his stay here.

It seemed we were getting a steady stream of mostly tourists from all over the world during the winter months, who all seemed to enjoy their time spent here. The cats, especially Mr. Peanut, were a big hit with most people, with the exception of one lady who complained of the "cat smell" in the house. I think she should have stuck with hotel room lodging for the sterile experience she was more comfortable with.

At work, I started to notice an increase in calls made by travelers wanting to cancel their flights, due to fears of a spreading virus called Covid-19. At home, the Gem and Mineral show—as it has done for years—attracted people from all over the world to visit Tucson for the big three-week event. I had received an inquiry from a lady in Michigan who saw my listing on Vrbo and wanted to stay for three weeks to attend the show. She offered to send me a decent deposit and pay in cash for the balance upon arrival.

Airbnb and Vrbo charged my customers a guest service fee and occupancy taxes. Let's say a guest stayed for six nights. They would pay the site $300 and my payout would end up being only $200. Some tech bros in San Francisco were obviously making a ton of money off this thing. So, I agreed to the Michigan lady's proposal.

When she arrived, she came with an air of entitlement. Judging by her bleached blonde hair and the way she carried herself, I think she was probably the head cheerleader in her hometown high school, twenty years and thirty pounds ago. As she handed me the cash, she said she had been sober all year, but now it was time to party. Oh boy.

On day one, I was out running errands when she called to advise me that the jacuzzi wasn't warm enough and I needed to turn it up. She then asked me for a staging area where she could post videos of her gem show finds to sell them on Facebook so I let her use my office space. She spent her days buying rocks and whatever else it is these people are into and each day piles of the stuff would cover every surface in the room. At night, she would cook steak and mushroom dinners for herself and proceed to get drunk before plopping herself in the jacuzzi.

In our conversations prior to her arrival, I had told her smoking was not allowed in the house, but we agreed to let her smoke her cigarettes on the porch. After finding a series of overflowing ashtrays left near the cat food bowls on the wooden desk on the porch, Janet confronted the "blonde blimp" by calling the cigarette smell disgusting. This led to a tersely-worded text from the blimp, so I had to be the mediator.

One night while I was trying to relax in the casita, I heard a banging noise out by the jacuzzi. I came out to see what the fuss was about and saw her buck naked, white ass struggling drunkenly to put the hot tub cover back on and then flipping a towel around her steamy pink back, as she trotted across the deck back inside the house.

One morning, I noticed a stick of butter on a small plate by the toaster, so I put it back in the fridge. That afternoon it was back in its spot with a note attached that read, "Please leave my butter out. I prefer it warm." From then on, I joked with Janet that the gem show had a new sponsor—the American Dairy Association.

As time went by with this lovely guest, Janet and I started to count down the days for her check-out date. I was cleaning the jacuzzi one day and noticed brown clumps on the bottom of the hot tub. At first, I thought they might be turds. On closer inspection, it turned out to be mushrooms. I asked her if she knew how they got there and she replied that she had no idea. Towards the end of her stay, as we crossed paths, I'd ask her when she was going to start shipping out her parcels of rocks. She would reply, "Soon, I'm still buying more."

Finally, the day before her departure, she realized the post office would not come to the house to pick up the boxes as she had assumed and a few frantic phone calls were made. She persuaded a friend of hers to pack them into their SUV. She didn't even lift a finger to help load them. After she finally checked out, I noticed dozens of empty vodka bottles in the bedroom closet and empty cans of her beer of choice, Natty Daddy malt liquor.

Another gem show guest from Texas who was staying upstairs in a balcony room during the same time was no trouble at all. He was looking for stones to use for arrowheads on his handmade arrows. He left days earlier than scheduled, didn't ask for a refund and even gifted me a used Charles Mingus record as he said goodbye.

After March 2020, the Airbnb bookings slowed down and things at my job were changing fast. The pandemic was beginning to take a toll on air travel and tourism in general so the airline decided to discontinue the home-based worker program. Since they had sold the building their employees once occupied as a call center in Tucson, an offer went out to all Tucson employees to either move to Phoenix to keep their job or take a buy-out package. If we took the buy-out, we'd have to wait until spring of 2021 for the lump sum. They gave us thirty days to make a decision.

I was about a year from my own planned retirement day anyway and I was almost old enough to collect Social Security, plus a modest monthly pension from the airline, so I opted out. I couldn't see myself living in Phoenix, a city I generally disliked, and I didn't exactly love my job since I was mainly tasked with lost baggage inquiries (not the happiest of customers) and endless refund requests due to Covid-19. I was now officially a retiree.

Janet decided to return to Seattle in April to be closer to her sons. We had developed a nice friendship and helped each other maintain our respective sanity. It was sad to see her go, but I can't say I can blame her in the least. With Trump's mishandling of the response to the pandemic as it grew more ominous, being near family was important.

I had placed an ad for new tenants on Facebook Marketplace, since the Airbnb hustle was practically non-existent by the spring. I did have one booking from an interesting Native American guy my age who drove in from Santa Fe to attend an Indigenous Conference held in Tucson. He told me his wife was scared to leave the house because she was terrified by this new epidemic.

Ashley, a girl in her twenties, answered my Facebook ad and soon moved into the loft space that Janet had vacated. She was working at a local nursery. She had a cat named Bean, who was even more antisocial than Mulrooney. Soon I noticed Ashley was getting fairly frequent visits from her boyfriend Tony, who was bringing over his loads of laundry and, more often than not, spent the night. I had to tell her if this was becoming a regular thing, I would have to charge her more for double occupancy and soon Tony had officially moved in. He was working as a driver for DoorDash.

In May, a Korean American young man named Jim Kim rented two rooms from me, a balcony room for sleeping and the downstairs office for studying. The latter room was curtained off near the spiral staircase, so if you wanted privacy, you'd have to be pretty quiet. He was also doing Door Dash deliveries for a short while, using a friend's car. For some reason, he wasn't allowed to drive. He had just gotten a job at a call center and was hoping to be able to transition to work remotely. I gave him some tips about call handling and phone etiquette, based on my job experience. He was working long hours, but still seemed to be broke most of the time. He subsisted on a steady diet of Flaming Hot Cheetos and Mountain Dew with the occasional Hormel "heat and serve" beef stew entree, topped with a generous mound of Flaming Hot Cheetos. I never saw him eat anything else.

I finally got an Airbnb booking that summer, a guy from Chicago who was a stand-up comedian. He invited Jim and me to Laff's, the local comedy club that had just reopened as Covid restrictions were loosening up a little bit. It was nice to get a few chuckles for free.

Janet had referred my rental space to a vagabond friend of hers named Amy Gee. She had worked with Janet at a Seattle bookstore and recently had been living in Mexico. She was looking for some frugal accommodations with good wifi so she could work from home as an English teacher. Amy arrived in July and was quiet, smart, and cheerful. She became a real asset to the household. With a strong Chinese work ethic, she volunteered her free time to help organize the kitchen and other parts of the house that were cluttered, plus helped me in starting a compost pile in the yard for future gardening ideas.

Airbnb also brought us this indie-film actress whose first words on arrival were, "Where's the nearest liquor store?" She was a bit of a wild card and ended up breaking a lamp, which she mentioned casually on her way out the door. My friend Bruno was quite enamored by her, but before he could try and make his move, she was long gone.

Things with Jim Kim were getting weirder. His employer had set him up with a computer, so he started to work from home. One time, as Tony was coming down the staircase, he caught Jim peeing into an empty water bottle while sitting at his desk working. When asked about it later, he said he was afraid he might get fired if he took a bathroom break. Amy Gee had her own opinion about Jim Kim:

"The young Korean guy, though very kind and polite, seemed to leave a literal trail of disaster behind him. He would drop food and drink wherever he went. His dishes alone kept the kitchen sink perpetually full. I walked into the living room one morning to find all the contents of a bag of potato chips exploded onto the carpet! The list could go on. Both Bill and I tried talking to the kid several times about being more respectful of communal areas, but a slew of personality disorders was his excuse for not remembering to clean up after himself. Bill was so frustrated for a while and eventually had to nudge the guy along to find a new place. He left peacefully, though Bill and I had to do a lot of the damage control afterwards."

One afternoon, I saw a little square ziplock bag of white powder fall from Jim's pocket onto the floor. He of course denied it was his. No wonder he was having trouble paying his rent. I had to ask him to leave. This didn't sit too well with him and luckily, Amy stepped in to try and diffuse the situation. I gave him another couple of weeks to get his shit together, but it wasn't working out. I helped him to find a seedy hotel in a sketchy area by the freeway that rented rooms on a weekly basis. It was all he could possibly afford. I even drove him there with his work computer and belongings in several trash bags. After he moved out, I had to clean his room. There were Flaming Hot Cheetos in every possible crevice—under the desk, the bed, the window sill, even inside the washer and dryer. I found one he had spat out wedged in the wall of his bedroom.

After that fiasco, we got a couple of decent tenants outside of Airbnb. Michael was a First Lieutenant in the Air Force. He was buying a house in town but needed a temporary place so he moved into the cheapest room—the downstairs office with the curtain barrier. It had a fold-down futon with an air mattress on top for extra comfort. He stayed until the end of September.

In August, Amy helped me with a one-day yard sale, held under the shade of the carport. From the leftovers from the record store, we sold t-shirts, posters, badges, comics, used records and more. We also had a rack of kaftans and dresses, plus a table of assorted costume jewelry from Julianna's personal collection—necklaces, bracelets, earrings, brooches and rings. The day was a nice break from the insulated Covid routine and it felt good to be part of the community, seeing neighbors and former customers from the store again. It was bittersweet of course to part with my late wife's things, objects that she treasured so much, but I'm grateful to have put them in the hands of people who will also appreciate them. Shortly after this, Amy decided to move on to Nebraska. It seemed Tucson didn't have enough to offer her when it came to an agrarian lifestyle she preferred.

A guy named Chase also got in touch with me about renting the other balcony room. His heritage was half Japanese and half Hawaiian, so he joked with me that he always felt conflicted on Pearl Harbor Day. He was moving to town from Chicago, had a job lined up working at a local coffee shop downtown, and was a big fan of Leonard Cohen and Bob Dylan. He seemed much older than his years, even fancied himself as a songwriter with his acoustic guitar. He was reserved and introspective but with a sharp sense of humor. We soon became friends.

One day stands out when an Airbnb guest named Yilin (a friendly young girl from China), myself and Michael were sitting around the dining room table talking about all the different apps there are in the world. SnapChat, Twitter, Tinder, TikTok, etc. I wasn't sure what Grindr was all about. Michael calmly told me it was, as he put it, "For the gays." Then Yilin said she was envious of my situation. She hoped that when she got older she would be living in an older house without the burden of a spouse or children. Michael said he agreed, and that he could do without the wife and kids.

For a couple of months, starting in October, a young man we'll call Atticus moved into one of the balcony rooms. He was working for Amazon, delivering packages to rural residents in southern Arizona, and was an activist for border rights in his spare time. I nicknamed him Antifa Atticus from Alabama.

There was relative harmony in the house with all the tenants getting along pretty well with each other. Airbnb brought us a couple of visits from Jeremy, who was working for the Arizona Conservation Corps, repairing trails and such on public lands. With this group, we had some interesting porch time, between Chase's guitar playing, Tony's attempts at poetry, and Ashley's nerdy sense of humor. Sometimes we would gather together at the dining room table for Phase 10 card games or Monopoly.

Another temporary guest we had in October was a goofy young man from Brooklyn, who showed up with a skinny Russian girl named Masha. I pointed out that the room was for a single person, not a couple. Ashley and Tony were convinced she was a prostitute, but as it turned out, she was just looking after her childhood friend who was autistic, to make sure he didn't get himself into any trouble.

I was living in the casita full-time now and rented out the master bed room in the house to a couple named Jack and Jill, whom I found via Facebook Marketplace. They were nice people, progressive in their politics, also involved in the Border Rights issues, but as it turned out, they would spend almost all of their time in the house, especially in the kitchen.

Between the two of them, they had one job, driving for Grubhub. One might be out driving, while the other would be cooking or baking. We're talking pork roast, deep fried food, pancakes, bacon, ribs, gravy, mashed potatoes, biscuits, the works. I'd come into the house to get my morning cup of coffee to find flour all over the kitchen floor, a sink full of dirty dishes, and a stovetop full of splattered grease.

Thanksgiving Day was interesting. Jack and Jill had made the customary holiday meal with all the trimmings, maybe an extra slab of pork roast thrown in for good measure. Between them, Antifa Atticus, Chase and me, we were all having a traditional family meal during Covid, minus the traditional family. It was also Chase's first time doing magic mushrooms, so the music he played on his guitar on the porch had that extra pinch of intensity that evening.

Jack and Jill seemed quite pleased with their living arrangements. When their ninety-day lease was about to expire at the end of December, they enthusiastically wanted to extend but I told them I was going to move back in the house. I was getting tired of sleeping in the ice box, my winter nickname for the casita.

They were nice people and all, but I wanted my house back, especially my kitchen. Ashley and Tony sometimes used the kitchen, but it wasn't a three large meals a day situation. With Atticus gone, the other three spaces were rarely unoccupied, but it was fairly uncommon for other guests to use the kitchen facilities.

Winter was always the busiest time for Airbnb guests. We had a mix of mostly single, equally female to male, from all ethnicities, savvy international travelers from various backgrounds and I was racking up quite a few positive reviews. Being a host meant taking care of laundry and housekeeping duties myself, and providing guests with a pleasant experience, so that their reviews would entice other guests to choose one of my rooms. Before I knew it, I actually became a Superhost! It was granted annually and had something to do with receiving mostly positive reviews and hosting a minimum number of reservations during the quarter. If you maintained status, once a year, you were awarded a $100 credit to use anywhere in the world on Airbnb.. When a guest checked out, I looked forward to seeing what they left behind. This usually supplied the pantry with a few eggs, peanut butter, a jar of mayonnaise, and a vegetable or two. Bottles of mustard and ketchup were common leftovers, as was Lawry's seasoned salt. At one point, I had four jars of the stuff! I accumulated enough guest leftovers that I started a "Communist Food Bank" basket, where others could take and leave assorted food items.

My favorite guests were the ones who were gone most of the day, working or sightseeing, using the space mostly for sleeping. Sometimes they would rent the bicycle, an idea I got from my stay in Amsterdam.

The Spiral Staircase

The Butter Incident (Art: Brian Walsby)

Loft Bathroom

Mr. Peanut reclines on porch

As I would find out over the years, it seemed that a greater percentage of the problematic guests were from Tucson. Their luggage was usually a large volume of Walmart plastic bags. They would tend to be less respectful of the space, and other guests. This included eating our food, leaving messes and poor communication. Were they floating around town using our home as temporary lodging in between evictions?

Towards the end of 2020, Ashley and Tony, who weren't getting along too well, moved out. Actually, she was the first to vacate. Chase and I were getting weary of hearing them bicker and argue. It got to the point where Chase asked me if he could move into the casita, to avoid having to hear their squabbles. Tony asked if he could stay a few weeks longer and I let him. When he finally moved out, he wouldn't return the keys. I asked him what the problem was and he told me to take it out of the deposit, which I had already given back to Ashley. I'm not sure what that was all about, but good riddance.

Another long-term tenant by the name of Coley came down from Show Low. He was a former U of A student, originally from Alta Loma, near my former stomping grounds of Pomona, and had worked as an EMT. I was shocked to hear they were paid basically minimum wage! He had a few horrific tales from that job experience that he shared with Chase and me, one involving a baby and a microwave. He was now using his Nissan Versa as a Lyft driver and took over one of the balcony rooms.

In March, 2021, Chase had found online a vintage 1984 Volvo he wanted to purchase. The only problem was, it was out in San Diego. I had just gotten my first Covid vaccine and hadn't been anywhere outside of Tucson in over a year, so when he asked me to drive him to California, I jumped at the chance. So, off we went, driving west on the I-8.

I had found an Airbnb near San Diego in El Cajon, that featured a teepee as a space to rent as one of their options. Nestled in Harbison Canyon, it was run by an eccentric hippie couple who lived in the main house. It had an outdoor kitchen and this eclectic long-term guest, real name was Bink Picard. His business card stated he was an artist, a cowboy cornucopia (whatever that's supposed to mean), craftsman, adventurer, and stuntman. Over a few beers, there were some entertaining tall tales—compliments of Bink—with the soundtrack of bullfrog croaks echoing off the canyon.

Chase took a standard room and I opted for the teepee for the night. I was kept awake by intermittent drops of water from a rare rain shower that dripped down onto my pillow from the open slot at the top of the tent. Luckily, the teepee came supplied with a plastic tarp that I used to cover myself.

Once we returned to Tucson with Chase's Volvo (nicknamed "brick" due to its squared-off boxy appearance) parked out front, Coley and I noticed a change in Chase's demeanor. He was more withdrawn, no longer joking with us, as was the norm. A few weeks later, Chase gave me notice of his intent to move out. He found a place just down the street from the house but would never visit us again. It was strange, as I had considered him a good friend during his stay here.

Coley and I bonded pretty well during his stay. He had a very analytical mind and questioned everything around him. He also had developed a strong kinship with Mr Peanut, after an incident involving a standoff between Peanut and a stray cat. Coley came to Peanut's aid, chasing the intruder around the house and giving him a swift kick that bounced the feral cat off an Airbnb car parked out front. From that moment on, a strong bond and mutual respect was felt between them.

In the summer of 2021, a girl we'll call Moana moved into the other balcony room across from Coley's. Initially, she said she was working at a nursery, then later it was Tohono Chul Gardens. It turned out these jobs didn't last very long and it became obvious she was earning a living as a stripper. She was a bit of a free spirit. As Coley put it, "She was banging half the guys in town," which led to his request to move into the casita.

As it was the peak of summer, no tourist in their right mind would want to visit Tucson, so short-term bookings fell off again.

I did get a regular guest, an aircraft mechanic that would drive in from El Paso for a four-day weekend, working a graveyard shift. His name was Qiheed, an African American Air Force veteran who was super easy-going and friendly. After doing a couple of Airbnb bookings—since we got along so well with easy small talk and such—he started paying cash for his bi-weekly visits. He did this throughout the summer and into the fall before he eventually retired from the job.

I rented out the bigger room upstairs to Rick, a hard-working Chicano landscaper who had a troubled past. He paid his rent on time and was hassle-free, at least for the first several months.

Coley and I started to devise a way to entertain guests with "a turd de Tucson" This was planned as a guided tour to be done in his Nissan Sentra with the two of us in the front, alternating as travel narrators to offer guests a glimpse of downtown historical (or was it hysterical?) highlights: OK Market, the abandoned Chinese grocery store on the corner, and the house that rumor has it Teddy Roosevelt slept in during a stop on his 1912 Presidential campaign. Newspaper accounts mention a lackluster speech in front of a bored crowd. A block away, was Ralph's Service Station which opened in the '50s, but was in business for only six months before it was abandoned for decades, the Five Points Arches with a statue of Cesar Chavez dwarfed by a much larger Ugly But Honest used car lot sign, the tail of a WWII era C-130 in front of a glassblowing shop, the old Synagogue built in 1910 (the first in Arizona) along with the Mexican Baptist church, the trendy Clifton Hotel that was once the site of a child's murder, - Saint Augustine Cathedral, the alley where Coley once witnessed a blowjob being performed in broad daylight and the Convention Center, where a thriving Chinatown was demolished during the period of "urban renewal". Nearby was the equally ugly TEP building, where the once iconic Santa Rita Hotel, home to movie stars and other celebrities was demolished to make room for the headquarters of the local electric utility. From there, the deluxe version of the tour would head towards the University and would include the 4th Avenue tunnel and the giant Rapa Nui statue that was salvaged from Magic Carpet Miniature Golf in 2008 and placed by a sports bar housed in a Quonset hut.. Coley would complete the narration once we were inside the grounds of the University, concluding with the site of a crashed Air Force jet that killed three people on the ground in 1978 (and narrowly missed Mansfield Junior High which was in session) a block from Wildcat stadium. We gave the tour to only one guest, a lady from Portland, who found it amusing.

In August, Moana threw a birthday party for one of her close friends. I think she invited only three people, but boy, was it a doozy! They all got very drunk in the jacuzzi area. Moana's friend's boyfriend began threatening to commit suicide and pulled out a gun. A shot was fired and the police showed up.

Coley came into my room and woke me up at 4:00 a.m., saying the cops were banging on his door asking where the gun was. I went out to talk to the cops. I saw a half-naked girl lying flat on her back by the curb, yelling and cussing at the cops, as they were taking her boyfriend away. In the carport was Moana, blacked out and covered in buzzing mosquitoes, sitting in the driver's seat of my car with its door open.

We had one guest in the office room at the time, a young girl in her twenties, who left her freaked-out version of that night in her review on Airbnb:

"Bill was very polite and helped me out a lot and I'm very thankful I was able to stay for two weeks to get on my feet as I moved here to Tucson from Iowa. If you want privacy, look somewhere else. There are a few people that are in the household and there is only a curtain for a door. I didn't mind. I appreciated the stay but the reasoning behind my rating was because of one night that scared me terribly. I was getting back to the house since I went downtown for an hour and saw a bunch of kids in the hot tub located next to the bedroom windows. They asked me if they were keeping me up with the birthday party going on and I said no (of course but I didn't want to ruin a birthday). I started watching a movie when I was in my room. I heard a loud noise and a girl screaming "omg what did you do" over and over again. I was so worried, I peeked through the window to see if everything was okay and everyone ran. I got nervous having no lock. I got up and went to the kitchen to do the dishes. I saw a girl run inside with her phone on speaker, freaking out. I figured if she went inside I was okay to leave so I made my way to my car by leaving the front entrance and I saw a girl laying on the ground completely out with just her swimsuit on. My heart dropped wondering why any of her friends were okay leaving her like that. I tried to help her up but she didn't. I saw these guys who were sitting in the truck get out and they said something I couldn't make out. I ran to the bathroom and locked the door because I didn't know what was going on. I waited 10 minutes and went back to the front gate and they put her in a car in the front entrance driveway with the driver seat wide open. Why didn't they stay with her, why didn't they keep her close? I didn't know what happened but I was so worried they did something to her but I wasn't trying to find out. I called a friend and stayed somewhere else that night because I was terrified and overwhelmed. It's not Bill's fault, but for a private experience that was a lot to handle right away moving here on my own. If you stay here a couple nights they don't hover and I love that. Just stay safe"

Not sure how I slept through most of that night. Might have been the noise of the A/C and fans blowing. Of course, the next afternoon, Moana was all embarrassed and apologetic. In hindsight, I should have asked her to move out, but she begged me to let her stay and promised it would never happen again. The rest of the summer and most of the fall was relatively calm. I was wary of having guests when I was out of town. If I planned a trip, I could block the calendar from being booked by guests. If anything went awry, I would want to be there to take care of it. There was a young girl who booked a balcony room. She seemed nice and all, but right before she checked out, she dyed her hair in the shared bathroom, leaving stains on the rugs and towels, plus multiple boxes worth of used hair dye supplies on the sink, not bothering to dispose of them. There were also hair dye stains in her room but the real kicker was when we discovered all of our cleaning supplies were completely wiped out. She used all of our bleach, vinegar, cleaning sprays and such. She must've thought I was a glutton for punishment and asked to book with us again a few weeks later, which I declined.
I had submitted some applications for employment in July. I was thinking if I could find something in the hospitality industry, maybe I could benefit from some employee discounts at hotels. I already had flight benefits from being an airline retiree but finding affordable lodging for these trips was always a challenge. It was my hope to find the missing link that would make travel easier on the pocketbook.

Much to my surprise, a manager at a Hilton property called me in for an interview. I sat down with her and we went over my job experience (a lifetime of customer service, both in retail and with the airline), what positions were available (housekeeping, front desk, janitorial), pay (minimum wage) and benefits (basic, minimal). She asked what I was looking for in a job. I told her that I wanted to work as little as possible and wasn't interested at all in climbing the career ladder. I told her I didn't really need the job or the money, I was retired but wanted to get out of the house a little and that I was reliable. Oh yeah, I wouldn't be able to start for a month.

She paused for a second, then told me it was getting hard to find workers, especially after Covid. Prospective employees would schedule for an interview, get hired, and then they would often not even show up. She also told me the one other benefit that might be attractive to me is the deep room discounts at all Hilton properties worldwide, even for workers that came in just once a week. I asked her what she had for just one day a week and she gave me the options. I took the job—a position at the front desk. 7:00 am to 3:00 pm on Wednesdays only.
I hated getting up that early and wasn't crazy about the job. I might have opted for the overnight shift, but that involved running an audit for the night and I hated math even more, so that was out. Too much time on my shift was spent staring at the computer screen and listening to mostly petty complaints from the hotel guests, but I really liked having six days off a week.

I had planned on taking a trip to Alaska for some time. I had heard that my friend Jeff and his band the Hickoids were doing a few shows up there, so I thought I would surprise them by showing up at one of their gigs. I flew standby from Tucson to Seattle, spent the night at the Seattle Airport Hilton and flew into Anchorage the next morning. I spent the night at another Hilton then rented a car in the morning for a drive west, towards Homer.

I had reserved a yurt on Airbnb in Soldotna, near Kenai, where the Hickoids were supposed to perform. However, I found out near the start of my trip, back in Seattle, that their tour was cancelled. I was bummed but I still wanted to see Alaska for myself.

The drive was filled with spectacular scenery once I got out of the big city. I didn't see any moose or dog sleds, but plenty of snow-capped mountains, spruce trees, and roaring rivers lined with fishermen. The yurt stay was kind of a let down—extremely cheesy, complete with a stuffed teddy bear staged on a rocking chair in the room. Not what I had expected but just being near an actual river was exciting for a desert rat like me.

The drive from there to Homer was a pleasant one. I stopped by an old wooden Russian Orthodox church on the way to Homer, which was a beautiful coastal township. I got a room at Lands End, a weather-beaten old-school resort at the end of a strip of land that was surrounded by the ocean that was called the Spit. I ordered the king crab for dinner, but was disappointed to hear from the waitress that it was imported from China. I've had better crab at my local casino in Tucson. Driving back to Anchorage for my flight home, I knew I wanted to see Homer and more of Alaska again.

In late May, I flew to Sarasota, Florida to visit my niece Paula whom I hadn't seen in many years. I owed her much gratitude in helping me with moving my mom from her apartment to Tucson in 2008 as dementia began to take its toll. Paula, who lived in Huntington Beach at the time, helped clear out much of the mountains of clutter, mostly piles of junk mail/solicitations from various Christian organizations. It certainly lessened my load when it came time to load the truck.

Since then, in her effort to find more affordable housing, Paula had moved first to Desert Hot Springs and eventually to Florida. I took a bus from the airport south to Venice, where she currently lives. The bus ride ended at the old Venice train depot, a prime example of Florida's Mediterranean Revival architecture. It was built in 1927, initially to make it easier for people to settle in the area. From 1960 to 1992, it was used to transport animals and equipment for the Ringling Brothers and Barnum & Bailey Circus, whose winter headquarters were in Venice. Once it closed in 1993, it fell into disrepair, until 2002, when it was renovated as a museum and bus depot.

Paula picked me up there and we had a good weekend visit, including dinner at Pop's Sunset Grill. She took me kayaking on a river to Manasota Beach, which was fun but challenging, as drunk boomers in their speedboats dominated the river traffic. I didn't see any alligators or manatees, but I got a good workout.

For several months, I had noticed a person on my social media feed would be the very first to "like" a post of mine. It occurred every single time. I didn't recognize from her profile pic if we had ever met in real life and eventually, out of curiosity, I sent her a private message. Even with the constantly revolving house guests and roommates, I was still feeling pretty lonely.

From there, we started chatting regularly and, long story short, we developed a relationship. Actually, this one was rekindled from one that had flourished briefly some twenty-five years ago, during a period when Julianna and I had split up. Sara and I initially met online and then in person back in 1996, in her home state of Minnesota.

After a few months, we broke it off. Julianna came back into my life and eventually Sara got married herself. A quarter-century later, in October 2021, we met up in Houston and just clicked. It was as if all those years of separation melted away. We both loved classic movies, live music and travel, even though our tastes differed somewhat, she was open to exploring new things. We met up for another weekend in Phoenix for a ZZ Top concert and then, a bit later, we had a nice Bay Area weekend that involved strolling in Golden gate Park and visiting my old Yippie friend Dan at his home in a small town in Marin County. He took us to see some magnificent Redwood trees. We also had another cat-sitting opportunity at Deanna's house in Berkeley.

I knew I was lucky to be able to work at the hotel with its perks of cheap lodging. It was nice to have someone to actually share that with, who loved to travel as much as I did. I now had some free time, as long as I was back in town for my Wednesday hotel clerk gig. As time went on, Sara shared more with me about her personal situation, namely being stuck in a progressively unhappy marriage for some twenty odd years. In November of 2021, she bravely took the next big step in her life and decided to leave her husband in Texas and move to Tucson to live with me. We were both excited to start a new chapter in our lives.

In December, Sara had filed paperwork for divorce after getting a steady stream of harassing and threatening voicemails from her husband, which I received as well. After a few weeks of this, we got an unannounced visit from him when he drove in from Houston, and pulled up in front of the house as we were about to take a bike ride. He insisted on Sara getting in his car to discuss matters. I was afraid she wasn't going to return, but eventually she was dropped off later that night.

The next day, while I was at work at the hotel, I grew concerned when Sara didn't answer my texts. I called the number of the soon-to-be ex-husband and that's when he told me he had taken her phone away from her, they were driving back to Texas and that I would never see her again. My heart sank, as I could hear Sara crying in the background and yelling, "No, no, no!"

After that, he dropped off his rental car at the Tucson airport and was proceeding to the airline ticket counter, with Sara resisting his efforts. He brought out a set of handcuffs in an attempt to detain her, take her back to the car rental area, and drive her back to Texas. Luckily for Sara, in an act from a God with a sense of humor, his pants suddenly dropped to his ankles and he wasn't able to walk. Sara took advantage of the opportunity and broke away from him, running off to hail a taxi back to our house.

The next day, we walked over to the downtown Tucson Police Department a few blocks from the house and filed charges against him. We told them what had transpired at the airport and played back the nasty, threatening voicemails we had both gotten from him, so that they could be recorded and filed for evidence. The police had already received a report of an attempted kidnapping at the airport, which is a federal offense, and let us know there was a video of the incident (pants dropping and all) in the possession of the Tucson Airport Police. They advised us to file a restraining order against him. To top it all off, I found out that her ex was an employee of the same company I had worked for. Much to my belief, the criminal offender was a pilot for American Airlines, my former employer.

By January 2022, Rick was beginning to get on our nerves, as he was now frequently inviting his new girlfriend over for loud, nightly sex sessions. In spite of a few requests to tone it down, he neglected to acknowledge the problem.   By February, it became necessary to ask Rick to leave due to his inconsiderate behaviour. and he was given a thirty-day written notice to vacate. Coley had left to live at his aging aunt's house in Phoenix in December but planned to return that spring. Moana was still staying with us when Sara's ex drove out again in March to drop off her wiener dog, Chloe. This time we got some advance notice because he sent word via Sara's mom that he was coming to Tucson. He had to be in town for a mandatory court appearance.

Since we had the restraining order, we asked him (via Sara's mom again) to leave the pet carrier by the gate. On the Ring camera, I watched as he pulled up, brought the carrier to the sidewalk and then waited in his parked car. He was probably expecting Sara to be home but was surprised when Moana came to the gate instead to pick up the pet inside the carrier. We were very grateful to her for doing this for us even though she was counting down the days to move out. She had already gotten her own eviction notice, as we had grown weary of her bringing over so many guests to the house for sleepovers.

I had never owned a dog myself, having had cats for pets most of my life, with the exception of desert tortoises in Twentynine Palms. It took a while to adapt to the canine, but I found myself getting more and more attached to Chloe. I gave her the nickname of Dingo, or Ding for short, which evolved into Dingus. She was incredibly loyal to Sara, following her everywhere she went. My felines, Mr Peanut and Harry also adapted to cohabitation and eventually they would take naps with Chloe on the couch and even joined us for walks in the neighborhood, at least a block or so, before returning to the house. On August 20th, our beloved cat Mr Peanut passed away. During his twenty some years on this planet he was loved by so many humans. I believe he was part extraterrestrial and could read your mind. We knew he wasn't going to be with us forever, but it was so sad to see him go. Early in 2024 we added another feline to our household. We were warned upfront of his health issues, mainly a set of rotted teeth and gums, but also respiratory issues. In spite of this, he really was the top charmer at the animal shelter. We couldn't resist taking him home, something others had done, only to return him after finding out about his medical problems. Oh yeah, he also sneezed blood on occasion, but we dealt with it. Harry was in dire need of a new sidekick after Mr Peanut passed, so for a name we went with Larry. We then had the comedy team of Harry and Larry, plus their stepsister, Dingus. Lucky for us, the shelter paid for a complete tooth extraction a couple weeks after we brought Larry home. This trio of pets would drop to two one night when Harry disappeared. After we'd been back from a trip for a couple of weeks, we noticed our cat Harry, who showed up in our yard ten years ago, wasn't around. He'd been mostly an outdoor cat, but now he had been missing for three weeks.. We saw him in our yard on our Ring camera the day after we returned , but then he disappeared from sight. We hope he is doing well. Perhaps he hopped a boxcar to Abilene to go to trade school or is enjoying his afterlife adventures with Mr Peanut and Frooty. We wish him a pleasant journey, wherever he might be. You will live forever in our hearts, Harry!

Tucson, AZ - Larry gets some sunshine

Harry in his Go Kart, Tucson, AZ

Amsterdam, Houseboats

Homer, Alaska

Elektra waits for a call. Berkeley CA

Chase pauses at the Del Coronado while in San Diego

Part Two - Planes, Trains and Autobiography

On May 17th, 2022, Sara and I drove out to Santa Fe, New Mexico to catch the Meat Puppets, who were co-headlining a tour with Mudhoney. She was accustomed to rock and country concerts with assigned seating and such. It was her first punk- rock- related live music experience and her first time hearing live music in a small club, one called Tumbleroot Brewery. The next day we drove back home to catch the Meat Puppets and Mudhoney Tucson show and invited Linda Kite and her partner Jack to stay in the casita, as they were still doing merch for the Pups. We then took the Amtrak west and saw them a third time at the Regent Theatre in downtown LA. Due to band members contracting Covid, the Meat Puppets stopped playing as a band shortly after this concert, so unfortunately, we weren't able to become true Meat Heads. While in L.A., we went to Hollywood Forever, the final resting place of Burt Reynolds, Johnny and Dee Dee Ramone, and Mark Lanegan.

In July, the divorce that Sara had asked for was finalized. He got off pretty easy. No division of property was involved but he did agree to spousal support payments spread out over the next five years..We waited and waited for many more months as the court proceedings dragged on for the kidnapping charge. Rescheduled multiple times, first due to his lawyer getting Covid, with another delay because he somehow contracted typhus. Eventually the whole mess ended when he finally took a guilty plea deal two years after the incident at the airport. The court gave the offender a light sentence of one year probation.

Later that month, our friend Janet came for a visit. Unlike our typical Airbnb guest, Janet prefers our hottest months in Tucson. We took her to Nogales, Mexico for lunch at La Roca, with its white linen tablecloths and five-star service. As we crossed back into the Estados Unidos, Sara was interrogated by the border patrol agents, asking about her relationship with myself and Janet. They thought she might have been a drug mule, as she was acting "suspicious" due to her responses. This had more to do with her hearing impairment than anything else. We stopped at Madera Canyon on the way home, wrapped up the day with a coatimundi sighting, a wooden bear, a wooden Indian, plus a hummingbird or two. The next day, we also took the tram up Sabino Canyon and saw yet another coatimundi, my spirit animal!

In August of 2022, an opportunity opened up at the hotel. I switched from front desk to kitchen, taking a job called "Evening Social Attendant," that had me serving free beer and wine and preparing soup, salad, snacks, and cookies. The "social" was held only on Wednesdays and much to my delight, it was only a four-hour shift, from 3:00 to 7:00 pm. As an extra bonus, I was allowed to take home any food leftover at the end of the night. My dream job had arrived!

In September, I heard that Flipper was doing some dates with Mike Watt. Since the tour wasn't hitting Arizona and because Flipper has been one of my all-time favorite bands, we took the train to Camarillo for a visit with my sister Mimi and caught their show at a small bar in nearby Ventura. It was great to hear the band again, but I must say, as much as I respect Mike Watt as a bass player, he really didn't have the chops at being their vocalist. Just not enough snark to pull it off.

We left from Goleta the next morning, hot coffee and a breakfast sandwich in hand, with the Pacific ocean as far as the eye can see. A sense of calm kicks in after thirty minutes or so onboard the train, something I've rarely experienced on a plane. On September 22nd, while on a road trip, I dug deep into my family's history. Headed north from Tucson, we stopped in Phoenix at the Fifth Avenue Cafe for lunch on our way to Montezuma's Castle. In the late '50s, this coffee shop was originally Upton's Candy, which had several Arizona locations. My mom and two of my sisters worked here in the 1950s, hand- dipping chocolate candy in the back room and waiting on customers at the lunch counter in the front. My late sister, Curl, had her first child across the street at St Joseph's Hospital.

We love Seattle! On September 22nd we were happy to get away from sunshine and blue skies for some drizzle and cold air spent with friends. Many thanks to our hosts and excellent tour guides, "little" Bill Tuck and Janet Brown, with gratitude to Matt Brown for the MoPOP (Museum of Pop Culture) tickets. Bill took us to see Freddy, the Fremont Bridge troll. Yes folks, LSD use can improve your city.

From Seattle, we took the train for the thirty-eight hour ride to Minneapolis, passing through Spokane, Idaho and arriving in Montana on the first morning. It was snowing as we were ripping through Montana on the Empire Builder, headed right towards Glacier National Park. Amtrak accepted our bid for a roomette, so we actually slept through Idaho, ate a freshly made omelet and drank decent coffee in our room and I had my first ever hot shower on the train. Another night was spent passing through freezing North Dakota. We saw daybreak in Fargo, before arriving at the Twin Cities station.

This was my first time meeting Sara's family. Her dad, Lee picked us up and drove us to Minnetonka, where I met her mom Cindy, her sister Jennie, brother Chris and his wife Katie. Sara also got to meet her niece Rosie for the first time. We had a nice visit and I enjoyed the Minnesota hospitality.

After our return home, on a brisk October day, a bright red utility van and equally bright red trailer, emblazoned with the Kellogg's logo, pulled up in front of our house. "Taste What's New," the slogan shouted, to no one in particular. The driver, Toucan Sam, was a friendly chap. His parents had raised him in a circus, so the travelling lifestyle was in his blood. He would set up the trailer in Walmart parking lots across the country. He admittedly knew his job was hypocritical. Under the auspices of promoting charitable good deeds like school literacy, the Kellogg corporation handed out a few pamphlets while promoting some of the highest sugar- content junk food on the planet. He offered us free samples from the latest in the Kellogg's product line—a large box each of Strawberry Milkshake Frosted Flakes and Pop Tarts. Score!

Later that year, in November, we followed the legendary '60s Brazilian psychedelic band Os Mutantes for three shows. The first one was in Santa Fe at the weirdly wonderful acid-inspired adult playground Meow Wolf, then in Denver at the Bluebird Theatre, the same venue that Raw Power had played in 1994.

The next morning, we took the California Zephyr from Denver to Emeryville. This is Amtrak's most scenic route, as it winds itself right through the Rocky Mountains during daylight hours. I got off the train in picturesque Glenwood Springs, Colorado during a "five-minute smoke break," as was announced by Conductor Cody. I said to myself, even though I no longer smoke, "Why not?" I was the last one off the train at this busy destination and was taking photos above the station platform when I suddenly noticed the train moving. I rushed down the stairs, ran along the tracks as the smiling conductor waved at me from an open window.

The train sped up. I rushed over to the station, frantically explaining my situation to the unsympathetic attendant. Her response was, "Looks like you're buying a new ticket and spending the night here, unless you can beat the train to the next station." This had happened often enough that Amtrak employees jokingly named Glenwood Springs the "Twilight Zone."

I looked out to the street facing the small quaint town and saw no taxi waiting for me, or anyone at all for that matter. Sara was calling me, after seeing my futile attempt to outrun the train. I knew that she was, like me, in panic mode. I got on my phone, hoping to hail a Lyft driver in this tiny town, my mind racing frantically. As I waited for a response, I called Sara back to tell her I was trying to get to Grand Junction, the next stop for the train, some eighty-three miles away. Minutes passed like hours, when finally a driver pulled up.

My driver, Faruk from Montenegro, assured me we can make the drive to Grand Junction in time. Striking up a conversation, as I tried to calm down, we shared our personal histories. After discussing everything from world events, jingoism, and the benefits of psychoactive substances, lo and behold we saw the Zephyr chugging along as we zoomed down the highway going ninety miles an hour. It even looked like it was slowing down as we sped up. Bob Marley blasted from the car stereo, "Everything's gonna be alright." Pulling into downtown Grand Junction, seeing the anti-Biden and pro Trump billboards everywhere and the plethora of generic fast food chains, Faruk and I pondered why people live in places like this. His theory was because it's flat.

I casually walked through the tiny Grand Junction rail station like nothing screwy had happened. Ten minutes later the Zephyr pulled up and I got back on board.

The rest of the trip was comparatively uneventful, but full of pretty spectacular scenery, as we greeted the next morning in rural Nevada, moving onto the Reno station, passing through the Sierra Nevada mountains down to Sacramento and reaching our destination of Emeryville.

Lake Havasu City, AZ with Sara and Dingo

Artwork by Brian Walsby

Who cut the cheese? Harrod's, London, UK

New Orleans LA-City Park

After we got home from another relaxing cat-sitting stay in Berkeley, a week or so later we drove from Tucson to Pioneertown near Yucca Valley, where we caught our third Os Mutantes show. They were a fun band to watch and put on a good show. Portuguese is a beautiful language for this psychedelic stuff. We stayed in an Airbnb that night, which was a vintage travel trailer at the end of a dirt road, where we froze our asses off.

On our way home we spent a night at Lake Havasu and fooled some friends on social media into believing we were actually in London, as we posed for photos near the "English Village", the waterfront sightseeing area with boat tours, pubs, and the London Arms restaurant, serving fish 'n chips. I remembered hearing, as a teenager in Twentynine Palms, the news of the dismantling of exterior masonry from a bridge on the Thames and how a new bridge was built spanning the Colorado River, incorporating the English masonry between 1968 and 1971. It was a big deal at the time, bringing a piece of Jolly London to the Arizona border. Driving home on I-10, just after the rest stop past Tonopah, we stopped to visit the anchor-shaped D. Boon memorial on the site of his fatal car crash.

In late December, we flew to New Orleans. I wanted Sara to meet my niece Deb, who was still living there and we both were craving a cafe au lait and a beignet. Laissez le bon temps rouler!

Deb picked us up in her car. She was driving for Uber, but luckily for us, the meter was off. The first two nights we spent at a Hilton near the French Quarter that had the employee rate. We did the usual tourist things, like get dusted with powdered sugar while enjoying beignets at Cafe du Monde, caught some live music at the Jazz Museum and Preservation Hall. We also did a ghost walking tour one night and explored the World War II Museum.

We then spent a couple nights with Deb at her shotgun house in the Garden District, one was spent driving all around New Orleans looking for cardamom to complete our recipe for some hot apple cider in the chilly evening and "cowboy" coffee in the morning. Deb's version of coffee was light on the coffee, but loaded with butter and cardamom. In between her shifts driving for Uber, she took us to City Park with its moss-covered trees and NOMA sculpture garden. We boarded the Sunset Limited in the morning together, as Deb wanted to visit her family in California for Christmas.

Towards the home stretch, we finally met the elusive "Burrito lady" of El Paso Station. At first, it appeared she was a no-show, but as we wandered around taking a few pics near the platform on our fresh air break, I noticed a large crowd gathering near the fence. Keeping my eye on the train, (no repeat of my Glenwood Springs fiasco, thank you please) I got in line as the excited and hungry throngs chatted amongst themselves. She's been doing this public service for many years and has quite the following. At only three dollars a pop, the foil wrapped, warm green chili and potato wonders were flying out of her massive ice chest. Her only words were "How many?" and "God bless you".

The Amtrak staff all bid her farewell and got in a few hugs, before everyone boarded and we pulled out, headed towards the ugly border wall along the Rio Grande. Rumors were circulating in the queue that food was running low in the Dining and Cafe Car, so I'm glad she was there. Visiting the Cafe Car for a beverage, I asked the attendant if he got himself a burrito. He replied that he would never eat her burritos and that he heard they were made in her bathtub. Some Amtrak employees have the driest humor. All hail the Burrito Lady!

We got off in Tucson, in time for me to do my soup 'n salad gig. We had time to show Deb the Saguaro National Park, Gates Pass and take in a movie at the Loft. They dropped by the hotel and pretended to be guests and got a free meal. We then boarded the Thursday night train to Los Angeles's Union Station, then on to Camarillo.

My other niece Cass picked us up at my sister Mimi's house. We all went out to Ojai for a sunny December lunch. After dropping off my sister, we headed up the mountains, to the top of Topanga canyon, where Cass lived in a small rustic rental cabin overlooking Los Angeles and the blue Pacific. From her wooden deck outside, you could see the Los Angeles skyline and planes taking off from LAX. In 1968 it might have been a smoggy Charlie Manson Christmas, with a Neil Young soundtrack (Revolution Blues, anyone?). However, 2022 was the year for clear skies and sharing love and laughter with the Delcastillos.

On Christmas Day, on our way to their father's house, (my brother-in-law Henry), we stopped in Long Beach, where we visited with their brother, my nephew Dan. First time I've seen him since the Meat Puppets show in Yucca Valley, November 2019. He's been in a rehab facility since a tragic motorcycle accident early in 2020, trying his best to recover from his severe brain injury. Dan struggled to speak, but his mom communicated by phone the best she could, as his sisters Cass and Deb and his brother Darren lent their heartfelt encouragement. If this isn't love, I don't know what is. I am blessed to be part of such a wonderful family.

Back at home, more guests came and went. Another Gem Show came with more interesting part-time tenants. While emptying his trash after he checked out, we discovered that a rock and gem aficionado from China wore disposable underwear. Seven pairs, one for each day of the week. I'm guessing it's part of the culture.

I received a booking from a former customer of the record store—a super music fan and live music enthusiast. Mullarkey stayed with us for a few days. I hadn't seen him in maybe ten years or more, so that was cool. We also had a guest from Bologna who was a nerdy U of A astronomy student. He was super friendly and fun to converse with. Sara and I took him out to the Gallery of the Sun and the Tucson Botanical Gardens on a balmy 110 degree day. We also drove out to explore Biosphere 2, blasting Neil Young and Crazy Horse during the drive. T-Bone in particular was a hit with the Italian. "Got mashed potatoes!".

My life as a punk rock innkeeper left little time for dull moments. In the not too distant past, I never figured this was what I would be doing in retirement, but I knew I was very fortunate in having the surplus income and a wonderful partner in Sara to help me.

Here's one of the more interesting reviews we got on Airbnb:

"Gloriously non-standard, and all that entails. This is a place where zine culture never died and underground sensibilities reign supreme. A DIY pirate radio vessel dropped into a historic neighborhood. From the esthetic alone, you might think that Bill, the host, would be a sneering punk—a brash and loud character with all the charisma of a drill sergeant. Wrong, bucko! He's a laid-back, affable dude and a gracious host. What else can you expect? How about fast, reliable wifi, a clean kitchen and your own half of a private balcony. Of course, there are challenges, but you're up to the task. You can navigate the weird bathroom situation, the spiral staircase and the delicate dance of sharing space with other guests, the host and some pets. For the low rate and the location, you simply can't do better in Tucson. Get ready for a memorable stay; this one's a wild ride."

In January 2023. Sara and I took a trip to the real London on a whim. We noticed American's non-stop flight from Phoenix had a hundred empty seats available, so we figured why the hell not? We were able to book an employee rate hotel room for three nights and did the non-rev thing. Blimey! After the ten-hour flight, it was quite cold with light rain when we arrived at our Paddington Station Hilton hotel on the Heathrow Express. We took a quick walk at a nearby park before catching a long nap to shake off the jet lag. The next day, after an amazing complimentary and truly complete English breakfast (not just the tea), we had a jolly good day (and night) chilling our bones, taking in the sights on a double decker bus in the rain, rubbing elbows with the idle rich and fashionista zombies at Harrods, and riding the tube to the river Thames. We ended the night at our hotel enjoying some British beef and fish n chips with my employee discount. Sometimes it's good to be a tourist! Spent the last day in London wandering around the city. Our fellow pedestrians spoke seemingly every language in the world but English. You got a lot going on, London!

In February 2023 we took a road trip to Yucca Valley to see the Hickoids play a gig on Super Bowl Sunday to a handful of people. I've always loved that stretch of road on Highway 62 between the Colorado River and Twentynine Palms, with nary a billboard in sight and nothing but pristine desert. Midway, we stopped in Parker, drove up the west side of the Colorado River, looking for elusive wild burros and saw the actual dam, where California steals all "our" water supply. The Hickoids were fun that night and we avoided the interstate as much as possible on the way home. We drove through Joshua Tree National Park to Box Canyon, with stops along the eastside shore of the fairly dystopian Salton Sea. In Mecca we stopped for a date shake, and then at eerie Bombay Beach, bizarro Slab City and Salvation Mountain for photos. Next stop, El Centro, the birthplace of Cher, and lunch at Sizzler!

In March 2023, my buddies in Raw Power were to play a single gig in Mexico City. Neither Sara or I have ever been to the capital of Mexico, so we thought it might be a fun quick trip. We tried our best to fly non rev, but there was a storm system impacting the flights from DFW, plus with spring break everything was sold out and non rev would've been impossible. We couldn't get out of either Tucson or Phoenix. We had a similar problem trying to get to Portugal a year later for another couple gigs that Raw Power were doing. Non rev is a crap shoot at times. Getting the employee rate at Hilton is also a limited availability deal, with Saturday nights always being the hardest to find rooms.

Not to be discouraged, we took a train trip instead to visit my sister in Camarillo, then down to Burbank. I lived here from 1960 to 1965 on Valencia Street. Staying at our friends Linda and Jack's place on this trip, I realized that my elementary school, Joaquin Miller, was only a few short blocks away, so why not explore the old neighborhood on foot? Digging deep into my childhood memories, I retraced the sidewalks I pounded as a youngster and found the same apartment building we lived in during my "formative years". Unlike several structures nearby, this one was fairly intact, exactly as I remembered it, except it seemed so much larger then. It was here where I played with my Lionel train set in my bedroom, and watched the news of the JFK assassination on our black and white TV. On the AM radio, I first heard the Beatles (whom I hated) and listened to the Cassius Clay (pre-Muhammed Ali) vs.Sonny Liston boxing match.. My older brother Mike and I lived in fear of making too much noise, as to not disturb our dreaded step-dad Jack, the xenophobic asshole from Texas. Our mom, as they say, did the best she could under the circumstances. We looked forward to visits from our older brother Ron, when he was on leave from the Army. One time, we took the city bus to "beautiful downtown Burbank" and caught a double feature of How to Stuff a Wild Bikini and Beach Blanket Bingo, preceded by Warner Brothers cartoons with chocolate candy and ice cream afterwards. It was one of my better Burbank memories.

While Sara and I were in Burbank, we had lunch at Bob's Big Boy, where the Beatles once ate after playing the Hollywood Bowl. We also took a tour of the Warner Brothers Studio and visited Buster Keaton's gravesite at the Hollywood Hills. Drove over the hill into Glendale. In 1965 that's where music on the radio got even better, as did television. Shows like The Monkees, Laugh-in, Batman, The Green Hornet, and F Troop all brought more color into our lives. It could've been worse.

My mom and stepdad had somehow decided converting to Seven Day Adventism was a great idea. We went to church on Saturday and became vegetarians, eating Loma Links and other soy based canned food. It was here in Glendale, where my older brother Mike and I were enlisted in the local Adventist "Academy". He was in 10th grade and I was in 4th. We had a two-bedroom apartment (which I found out still stands in 2023) just a few blocks from school, just off Chevy Chase Drive. On weekends, we would hike to the top of the hills above the canyon and look out over the smog-filled horizon. I liked the area and absorbed myself with the culture of the times, namely Mad Magazine, The Munsters, The Beverly Hillbillies and late night monster movies. Mike was trying his best to impress the girls at high school with his track and field skills and his Nehru jacket. We would also go to Griffith Park on some weekends and hang out. We even went to a Dodgers game (vs the Chicago Cubs) back when Sandy Koufax was pitching.

Before catching the train home to Tucson, Sara and I ate at Phillipe's near Union Station because I'd heard of this food joint that supposedly invented the French Dip sandwich. Nearby Olvera Street is all well and good for when you crave a Mexican platter, but we wanted to branch out a bit more. Since we had a three-hour layover before catching the Sunset Limited, I figured we'd give it a go. We knew we were on to something when we saw a line longer than the TSA check in at Sky Harbor. Turns out the hype is worth it. They have been cranking out affordable dips (single, double or wet) since 1908! Delicious! For the vegans, there's even the best pickled beets and baked apples I've ever tasted. Next time you're in downtown L.A., check it out.

Also in May, we took a road trip to San Diego. First stop was at Pete's Seafood for a lobster roll and then we had a nice visit with my cousin Sue and her husky dog, Roma in Oceanside. We spent time at laid-back Ocean Beach, had lunch at the snazzy, historic, luxurious Hotel Del Coronado and walked around rustic Old Town San Diego. We also had a short dinner visit with Daniel House and his wife Patty. He told me he was still working on his Skin Yard book.

The summer of 2023 involved some other fun trips. Later on in May, we took a trip west to see John Fogerty play the LA County Fair, which was a great concert. He was ecstatic to be playing his own CCR songs again after decades of legal hurdles. Hearty Har, a band featuring his two sons, opened up. You could tell he was having the time of his life. So great to see such pure joy in a performer.

On our way to Pomona, we stopped in Palm Desert and downtown Palm Springs. In Palm Desert, the weather was a nice, surprisingly cool and breezy day for summer, so we decided to take a stroll around the campus of my brother Mike's old school, College of the Desert. This was back in 1967 and the Vietnam war was in full swing. We had just moved out to 29 Palms from Glendale and Mike had just turned 18. The selective service offered a crappy birthday present, if you ask me.

To avoid being drafted, he enrolled in this college. Unfortunately, he was unable to keep his grade point average high enough and before we knew it, he enlisted in the Navy. Later, I heard stories of his days stationed at Pearl Harbor, goofing off with his pal and how the lucky sailors caught a Jimi Hendrix concert on Maui, plus the Chambers Brothers and some new limey band called Led Zeppelin. I found out much later he was involved in handling shipments of the highly toxic chemical Agent Orange, which may have led to his health problems later in life. He also lent a hand in scooping one of our Apollo astronauts out of the Pacific. He was proud of his time in the service and when he passed away in 2014, he was given a full military burial in Riverside. I still miss my groovy brother and think of him often.

While staying in Pomona, I decided to visit Matt "the Rat" Estel in Pomona. We had gotten in touch via Facebook a few years back, but hadn't seen each other in person for forty years. I first met him at Freaks Head Shop on Holt Avenue. Starting in 1979, we would take my beat up Toyota to Chinatown and Hollywood several times a week to catch punk rock bands. Some of the best times of my life. When we showed up at his Pomona home, he surprised me with a mountain of ticket stubs he saved from back in the day. It was great to catch up.

After our Pomona visit, which included the L.A. County Fair and the Fogerty concert, we dropped into Dr. Strange Records and to my surprise, Bill Plaster was actually there. Another person I hadn't seen in person in four decades, when he was just a young customer at Toxic Shock. He gave us some Dr. Strange swag and towards the end of our visit, mentioned he was working on a book. I thought to myself, I'll be damned if he puts a book out before I do and decided to get serious with getting mine published. I had been writing my memoirs for a few years at this point, but wasn't sure what I was going to do with them. This was the pivotal moment when I convinced myself it was high time to quit procrastinating.

Since I had no real experience in publishing, other than putting together mail order catalogs and newsletters for the record store, I contacted Matt Thompson at Fluke to see if he would be interested in helping me achieve my goal. He seemed to like the idea and said he would be glad to help. With new resolve, I finished up my writing.

Burbank, CA - Bob's Big Boy
Des Moines, IA - 80/35 Festival
Ojai, CA, with the DelCastillos (Cass, Deb and Mimi)

Salton Sea, CA - Slab City

Denver, CO - Union Station

Pigeon Forge, TN, with Paula Deen

In late June 2023 we took the Sunset Limited again to Los Angeles and visited my sister Mimi in Camarillo. It's important for me to visit as often as possible, as she is my last surviving sibling and she is now in her '80's. We spent two nights at Linda Kite and Jack's place in Burbank. Neil Young was doing a solo tour and we got tickets to one of his shows at the John Hanson Ford Amphitheatre on July 1st. It's a much more intimate version of the Hollywood Bowl, a cool amphitheater tucked into the hills, right next to the 101 Freeway. I was last here on April 22, 1988 for the Swans, during their Children of God tour.. Neil put on a great show of mostly deep cuts, a highlight for me was I'm the Ocean from his Mirrorball album.

The next day, Linda and Jack gave us a swell narrated tour of Hermosa Beach, where Black Flag has a deep history. We saw the Lighthouse, a jazz club once booked and operated by Ozzie Cadena, the father of the third Black Flag singer, Dez. We also walked by the "Church", featured in the first Decline of Western Civilization film, a strip of sidewalk along the beach called the Strand where you could get "Wasted with the burnouts and the hippies" as Keith Morris sang on the Nervous Breakdown 7", and Media Arts studio where Spot produced all the early SST bands when they put their songs on tape. We also ran into Bill Stephenson on our walk who complimented me on my Hickoids t-shirt. Of course, in 2023 Hermosa Beach is totally gentrified, but Linda, being a childhood friend of D. Boon, knew her shit. We got dropped off at Union Station for the train home.

In the summer of 2023, the Airbnb bookings slowed down again so we took in a renter via Facebook Marketplace for the bigger room with its own bathroom. It was a guy named Travis, who was a creative, artistic type, super-friendly and excited to move in, especially after he saw the anti-Trump sign in our front yard. He was on disability for something and said he was looking for work, but in the meantime, his mom would help him out.

When he came to the house to sign the rental agreement, he brought his mother, who had flown in from North Carolina. She had just bought him a used truck and proceeded to write me a check for two months rent in advance, plus the deposit. She also was asking about the mortgage and details of the relationship between Sara and me, a little too nosy, in my opinion.

Travis moved his stuff in and his mom flew home. One day we found a hair salon chair, complete with the plastic dome, out by the trash. Evidently Travis dragged it in from the alley and just left it there. A couple of weeks later, we got a message on Facebook from a friend of Travis, who was wondering if we had seen him. He was supposed to cat-sit for her and she hadn't heard from him. I had noticed his truck was gone and that he had left his air conditioner running in his room. His mom also got in touch with us, wondering if we had seen him lately. Shortly after that, his mom did a little more research and found out that Travis had been arrested for human trafficking outside of Tombstone and was incarcerated at the Cochise County jail. His friend arranged to pick up his things, so I went into his room to discover a total disaster area. Dirty clothes, a couple dozen thrift store kitchen appliances, uneaten food, dirty dishes, and half-full beverage containers were everywhere, plus a pile of rotten vegetables on the table. I helped his friend pack up his belongings. His mom was frantic to get any important documents that Travis might have left in the room. I found some stuff, including a letter from another county where he had a warrant for his arrest. After I mailed these to her, she started to haggle with me to get a refund for unused rent. She also asked me if I wanted to buy his truck. No thanks, lady!

Also in July 2023, we turned into Idiots Out Wandering Around. You guessed it, we were in Iowa! Digging that significantly cooler air, we ate Chinese pizza. (No, that's not a Neil Hamburger joke!) We were here in

Des Moines to catch House of Large Sizes at the 80/35 Festival. 80/35 is a cool downtown music festival that's been running for over fifteen years. The HOLS were also being inducted into the Rock and Roll hall of fame (of Iowa, not the one in Cleveland).   They took us to their favorite Thai restaurant before the show. That night, House of Large Sizes absolutely burned down the barn at 80/35 in front of a packed crowd of loyal fans that knew all the lyrics..So great to catch up with HOLS band members and friends Dave and Barb after a mere thirty years.   Later that month, we caught another Neil Young solo gig in Napa, Northern California and stayed with Peter Handl in Richmond. I recommend that whenever possible, take the ferry from Richmond (or Oakland, for that matter) into the city of San Francisco. It's a great way to get around. You can thank me later.

For Sara's birthday, we wrapped up a busy summer by flying into Seattle to celebrate the day with cake on Janet's balcony, overlooking the popular tourist spot, Pike's Place Market. The next day Bill Tuck picked us up at our hotel. Our first stop was Greenwood Memorial Park in Renton for the impressive Jimi Hendrix gravesite, then off to Snoqualmie falls, a joy for me to witness as a desert rat. During the drive, we crossed over many bridges and tunnels, stopped for lunch at Twede's Cafe in North Bend where the Twin Peaks TV series was filmed and visited Kurt Cobain's house and memorial bench. We went to another park with more tributes to Hendrix, saw Bruce Lee's grave, the Ballard docks, the Seattle skyline, more water and made a bridge troll revisit. Kudos to Bill Tuck for the excellent one-day whirlwind tour! We took Amtrak's Cascades south the next day to Eugene, where we had a great two-day visit with my niece Cindy and her husband Fred along the beautiful Oregon coast, spending the nights near the sleepy town of Yachats before flying home.

It's always great to escape Tucson for cooler climates during the summer months. Don't get me wrong, I love calling this city in Baja Arizona my home, in spite of the increasing gentrification of its downtown. I love the neighborhood I live in with the occasional visits from roving packs of Javelinas. It does seem however, that each summer gets just a little bit hotter and drier and the summer monsoons tend to disappoint. I'm grateful for having the free time, my friends, family and of course my soup 'n salad gig at Hilton. As long as I'm able to get home to work each Wednesday, I'm able to take up to six days to travel. I'm a lucky man to maintain this modern vagabond lifestyle and to have Sara here to enjoy it with me. I certainly don't take it for granted.

In September we began a journey consisting of trains, trains, automobiles and a doomed ocean liner. We flew to New Orleans, spending one night there before boarding the Crescent in the morning. This Amtrak route originates here and ends up in New York City two nights later. We had tickets to Greenville, South Carolina, to visit my sister-in-law Adrian and her husband Charlie. For this journey, we had a sleeper roomette, due to a bid up that was accepted. Meals are included when you get a sleeper, but on the Crescent, that's "flexible dining", merely a microwaved entree similar to a Banquet TV dinner, delivered to your room with the bare minimum of civility by a disgruntled Amtrak room attendant.

The Crescent uses single-level cars, much older than the Superliner, which we had grown accustomed to. It's not like the double deckers are really that much newer. There's been no real upgrades to those cars since the late 70's. The train starts out crossing a bridge over massive Lake Pontchartrain, which takes almost an hour. It then passes through Mississippi and Alabama, and reaches Georgia around midnight, scheduled to arrive in Greenville at 2 am. Adrian and Charlie were waiting to pick us up, but naturally we were delayed by two hours.

I wasn't sure of how awkward introducing Sara to Julianna's older sibling would be, but my apprehensions were in vain, as it all went very well and we had a lovely visit with my in-laws. We met up with their son Chris the next day and spent the day exploring downtown Greenville. The following day, after breakfast they drove us out to the Asheville airport in North Carolina so we could rent a car.

Our next leg of the trip was to meet up with Sara's family including her parents, sister and brother, his wife and Sara's niece Rosie who was just a year and a half. They had some cabins reserved at a Cherokee KOA campground in the Smoky Mountains and we spent a couple of days there having BBQs and such along a creek. I bought a coonskin cap at a roadside tourist trap. Just like Daniel Boone.

We passed by the Appalachian trail, on through Gatlinburg on our way to Pigeon Forge, Tennessee, where we had a fried chicken lunch at Paula Deen's and did a tour of the Titanic. Not exactly sure how this ill-fated ocean liner ended up here. We returned the car to Asheville and flew home. Thanks Louisiana, Mississippi, Alabama, Georgia. South Carolina, North Carolina, and Tennessee for your southern hospitality. Love your shrimp, biscuits, fried chicken, mussels, and grits, not necessarily in that order. Boiled peanuts, not so much.

Back in Tucson, we caught Ringo and his All Star band at the convention center on September 19th. To date, he's the only Beatle I've ever seen in concert. It brought back memories of how my sister Mimi once caught me loudly singing along to Yellow Submarine on the radio as a shy eleven year old boy. Her encouragement was a welcome respite from a somewhat repressed childhood.

October of 2023 turned out to be a great month for live music. On the 4th, we boarded the eastbound Sunset Limited to San Antonio and connected to the Texas Eagle north to Austin. During the day, we hung out with Bob Suren, Don Rock, and Tim Stegall, just not at the same time. Plus we record shopped at Waterloo and End of an Ear. I have been wanting for years to check out the Corn Lover's Fiesta, an annual event put together by Jeff Smith. This year, it was held at the club Sagebrush. Two stages were set up, so there was no wait between bands.

We had an absolute blast. The topper was seeing the Hickoids with the legendary Frontier Dan in front of a decent sized adoring crowd. We also became instant fans of the amazing Beaumonts, the charming Jane Woe, Alaskan goth punk from Cliff and Ivy, the scary Ghost Wolves, and loud rockers Pussy Gillette. One of my favorite bands from the late nineties Austin scene was the Fuckemos and that night we witnessed their reincarnation featuring the delightful crooning duo of Sean Wheeler (of Throw Rag fame) and the velvet- throated Russell Porter. For this night's show, they called themselves Fake Emos, but I was just happy to hear all my favorite Fuckemo classics, like 80 Gay Sailors and Lingerie Dreams. It was getting late, and we had to catch an early flight home, so we missed the headliner, Panther Burns. We had already bought tickets to see Cheap Trick at home, but we knew his tour was also coming to Tucson on the same day, the 11th, so the plan was if Cheap Trick finished their set early enough that same night at the Rialto, we would go across the street to Club Congress and catch the Panther Burns set. Lucky for us, that's exactly how it worked out. With a crack Italian backup band, Panther reminded me of a rock 'n roll Charlie Chaplin. He was kind enough to sign a copy of his newest album for me.

Shortly after that, on Oct 13th we did a road trip with Dingo to witness a desert rock eclipse at Taylor Junction in Joshua Tree. We wanted to see a new band outta Phoenix, Happy Universe. Linda and Jack came up from Burbank to make the scene, a night for something old, something new! Three of the Meat Puppets (Chris Kirkwood, Derrick Bostrom and Elmo Kirkwood) doing a brand new thing without their main songwriter Curt Kirkwood. Elmo did his best filling his dad's shoes on psychedelic lazed guitar. Chris did some of the Pups songs that he had penned and the band did some free form originals. Plus we were treated to some Salton Sea inspired poetry from Sean Wheeler. I also met Jay Martin, with whom we seem to have quite a few mutual friends, including Jeff Smith and Sluggo, to name a few.

From the High Desert, we drove out towards the Pacific ocean, stopping to pay my respects to my brother Mike at Riverside National Cemetery, then south to Oceanside for another visit with cousin Sue. Dingo enjoyed that immensely, as she got to play with Sue's husky, Roma. From there, we took in the sights and smells of Ocean Beach and had a little seafood at Pete's before heading to the Soda Bar in San Diego on the 15th for a great set of seminal UK punk from TV Smith and the Adverts! If that wasn't enough, at the AVA amphitheatre in Tucson by the Casino del Sol, we saw Alice Cooper put on a great show with all of his classics on Oct 21st. I've seen him a few times in the last ten years in his home state of Arizona and he always delivers the goods. His theatrics never get boring and his current band is solid as can be. Sara was quite impressed as well.

We got tickets for Devo Nov 16th at the You Tube theatre in L.A. The venue was too large for my liking and the seats weren't the best, with an awkward side view of the stage, but Devo was still pretty great. While in Los Angeles, we went to the Academy Museum of Motion Pictures, which had a cool John Waters exhibit. We also visited with my sister in Camarillo, arriving a little too early in the morning for her liking, so she let us borrow her car. I wanted to take Sara out to the place that put Camarillo on the map.. We visited Camarillo State Hospital today or "CAM" as it was named affectionately by its employees.

A scary place in a beautiful setting, many unexplained patient deaths happened here. Fifty male patients arrived in Camarillo in March 1933, and were initially housed in what was then a farm. That number grew to over one hundred by June 1934 and eventually grew to seven thousand patients, making it the world's largest mental hospital. Ever wonder where the term funny farm originated? This is the place.

Due to the hospital's proximity to the media center of Los Angeles, it has been referred to in movies, television, and music. Some famous people with mental illnesses, or ones who were detoxing from drugs or alcohol, stayed there to recover in Ventura County's mild climate. Jazz musician Charlie Parker's Relaxin' at Camarillo was written while he was there, detoxifying after a heroin addiction. The 1948 movie, The Snake Pit, with Olivia Dehavilland was partially filmed here. Frank Zappa had a song called Camarillo Brillo on the album Over-Nite Sensation. The punk band The Screamers, led by front man and artist Tomata du Plenty, gave a gig at Camarillo State Mental Hospital, inside the premises, for the benefit of the patients, on March 23rd, 1978. Shortly after that, it was immortalized in song by the band Fear on their debut album. The hospital grounds converted to a Cal State Channel Islands campus in 1998.

I had been in touch with my old friend Ed Colver in recent years via Facebook, or as he calls it, "so so media" . I was hoping to get his permission to use some of his photographs for my book project, specifically ones he took in Pomona, at the P.A.L. gym and in Riverside. He had invited me to pay him a visit, and since I hadn't seen him in 40 years, I figured the time was right. We went out to his charming Craftsmen house near Pasadena and spent a couple of hours hanging out on his back porch, drinking coffee and watching the squirrels in his heavily forested back yard. We scrolled through some of his incredible early 80's punk rock photographs on his tablet and he let me pick out a few to use for my book. We went to the Norton Simon museum afterwards and then had lunch with another dear friend, Bob Durkee, before driving home to Tucson.

On December 7th 2023 we were in Denver, famous for omelets and for tonight at least, a tasty Tuna melt at the Paramount Theatre. The last time I saw Jack Casady on stage was at the Whisky when his band SVT opened for the Dead Kennedys in 1980. Not all hippies are burnouts. This was billed as the Final run of Hot Tuna Electric. I guess amps are too heavy to lug around as you age gracefully.

The next day, we had a brisk afternoon exploring the city on foot. We saw the Capitol Building, the Molly Brown house, the legendary Wax Trax Records and the equally impressive state history of Colorado Center, a worthwhile winter walk. We boarded the California Zephyr from Denver's Union Station the next day, heading west. This is our happy place, climbing up the Rockies from the mile-high city.

On December 9th, we were at the Glenwood Hot Springs Lodge and pool, although we didn't stay at the actual lodge, as we had a far cheaper motel within walking distance.Overlooking the hot springs is the Colorado Hotel, once considered Teddy Roosevelt's western White House, as he loved spending time there, between hunting and fishing.

We had been here the summer before, when the pool was packed to the gills with kids splashing in the pool and screaming on tubes down the water slide. We had opted for another, smaller adult-themed hot spring farther up the river instead. This time the slide was closed for winter. We checked it out, as thousands have done since 1860, and I definitely saw the appeal. The large pool (world's largest at that) is pretty darn warm at 94 degrees while the smaller one is hot as advertised at 104 degrees, a pleasant escape from the air temperature of 10 degrees.

It was kinda surreal as steam rose from the mineral water in the dark and bodies of all shapes, sizes, ages, and ethnicities floated by. It was a rightwing conservative's worst nightmare. When we exited, we looked like steamed lobsters.

In daylight, we appreciated our surroundings, the blue sky, snow-covered mountains and ancient brick architecture. If it was good enough for Teddy Roosevelt, Buffalo Bill, Doc Holliday, Al Capone and Ted Bundy, it was good enough for us! A special place indeed.

I had been working steadily on my writing, putting my memories together, and I was fairly pleased with the work I had accomplished. Now it was time to get serious on how to illustrate them. In October of 2023, I started digging through my own photographs, ticket stubs, gig flyers and such.

I've never been a particularly organized archivist of my own history. Things were scattered in various parts of the house and garage. It didn't help that a great deal of my documents related to the history of Toxic Shock were consumed in a house fire in 2010 that wiped out much of my flammable archives in the attic. I also found a number of images online that corresponded with my life events and got in touch with friends and acquaintances to help me to fill the void. It was important for me to fill my stories with photos and other images. I didn't see any sense of the photos and mementos hiding away in a drawer when they could be seen by others who might appreciate them. On the rare occasion when I read a book all the way through, it helped if it had more than just text filling the pages.

You could say I had a somewhat of a short attention span. Being raised on television, I was really more of a magazine or music fanzine reader than novels and non-fiction, although I did enjoy poring through history books.. I often got bored with reading a book that was just all text, and would seldom finish it. There were exceptions of course, the writings of authors like George Orwell, Jim Thompson, Ed Abbey, and of course John Henry Toole's A Confederacy of Dunces.

I also enlisted the help of artist Brian Walsby to design the book cover artwork. I had seen his work as far back as the release of 7 Seconds' Walk Together, Rock Together album back in 1985 and found his comic strips in assorted fanzines that lampooned various punk scenesters pretty amusing. I sent him a photo image of the shop with the Toxic Shock sign from our original location in Pomona and asked him to add some pertinent band logo graffiti to the blank wall of the building. He asked me why I didn't want to include my own image on the cover as well, instead of just a building. I let him make a caricature of my headshot from the late 80's. Brian was really good at simple line art caricatures, so I told him to go ahead. I was pleased with the result and the speed in which he delivered it, so I also asked him to put his mark on several band photos that the Toxic Shock record label had worked with over the years.

Working with Matt Thompson at Fluke, sorting through a life's worth of memorabilia to include in a biographical book was becoming an arduous process. He was laid off from his job and had some free time to tackle the project. I was paying him by the hour to proofread my writing and incorporate my graphics with the text.

I soon realized this was taking much longer than I had expected. I thought it would be great to have it completed by December of 2023, but soon realized that wasn't going to happen. About a month in, we had the first chapter illustrated but I had nineteen more chapters to go. We decided instead to target March 20th, Julianna's birthday, as the official release date.

The book editing process was tedious and frustrating, deciding how each page should look. Sara and I drove up to Phoenix, hoping to speed up the process by working with Matt in person for a couple days instead of through a series of emails. Doing that helped a little, but still there was much more to do.

Matt was taking a trip to Europe for a couple weeks and asked us to take his young cat Sukoshi back home with us so he wouldn't need to find a cat sitter. We agreed, thinking Harry might enjoy the feline companionship. The idea was to get more in-person work on the book done at our house, after his trip was over.

Sukoshi earned her nickname Nagasaki Nightmare by literally climbing the walls and going into heat. Harry would have nothing to do with her and Dingus wasn't a fan either. We had been careful to keep her inside so she wouldn't escape but when Matt came back to Tucson to retrieve her, one of the first things he did was open our front door wide. Sure enough, Sukoshi ran right out the house, down the porch and scampered off, down the alley. Instead of working on the book, we spent most of the afternoon roaming the neighborhood trying to find her. The book project went back to working around Matt and his family's schedule, getting it done in bits and pieces, between school functions and sporting events.

After months of back and forth emails, Matt and I finally had put together a version of the book I was happy with and we sent the digital master off to the printing facility outside of Chicago. I had found the sweet spot number of 1500 copies that brought the per unit price down low enough to make it potentially profitable, that is, if I was able to sell them all. I was footing the bill for the entire project, including paying Matt a premium for all the necessary pre-production work. I wanted to keep the book's retail price affordable at twenty dollars. To do that, we had to keep the page count to around two hundred and it was necessary to shrink the size of the photos, if I wanted to have them all included.

When the day came for delivery of the book to my home address, Matt drove down from Phoenix and we waited for the Fedex truck to arrive on March 29th, 2024. It was exciting to finally have an actual finished product in our hands. Sara, Matt and I helped the truck driver unload the thirty-eight boxes and the driver was grateful to have the assistance, as they were quite heavy.

We cracked one box open and flipped through the pages of my first book.. At first Sara was a bit taken aback by the abundance of photos and references to Julianna. It must be an awkward position for her to live in the shadow of another important woman in my life. I tried my best to explain to Sara that this book was indeed a tribute to her and to reassure her that although this book documented my history, she was now the most important woman in my life and would continue to be in the future.

Overall, I was happy with the book's content, but I did notice some images were a bit fuzzy and hard to see, the Walsby band cartoons in particular. Some pages that had ghost images in the background obscured the text. These details weren't all that apparent in the digital world, but when translated to actual paper, they became fairly evident. But considering it was our first effort at DIY publishing, I was still pretty damn proud of it. I figured some people might appreciate the effort, and it would probably take me a few years to sell them all, but it was well worth it to me, to get my story told. After unloading, we went to Rocco's Pizzeria to celebrate.

Seattle WA with Bill Tuck
Yucca Valley, CA

The book arrives
(just kidding these are the No Values zines)

Tony Adolescent checks out a copy

Dr. Strange Records, CA

Wooden Tooth Records, AZ

Berkeley CA - Long Haul with Deanna Ewers and Janet Rogers (photo by Gil Warquez)

No Values Festival

Zoinks! Records

Matt the Rat brings out the cake at my birthday E
photo by Katrina Walker

Once I got the word out on social media that the book was available at last, we got plenty of direct mail orders for it and that kept us busy taking trips downtown to mail them off. One day, a new clerk at our local post office got annoyed with me for the sheer volume of book parcels we brought in to mail, and kept letting her other customers in line cut in front of us. After thirty minutes of this, I explained that I had come to this same location for three decades and often had to wait in line myself, which I accepted as a mere inconvenience. I further explained that a mailing this large was a rare occurrence for me. She got even more upset with me and as we finally wrapped up our business, made a snarky comment about how I must think I'm "all important". The regular clerks didn't cop this same attitude. They casually asked what I was mailing and when I told them, they were happy for me. One actually slipped me a twenty dollar bill and bought a book.

Times had changed quite a bit since the days of running a record label. I was finding it difficult to find a distributor to take on the book, not that record distribution had been that easy in the first place. It involved plenty of time spent chasing wholesalers for payment (or returns) plus direct mail order sales and trades with other labels around the world. Microcosm (an indie book distributor in Portland that I had dealt with many times as a retail store in the past) asked for an advance copy. After reviewing it, they told me they didn't think a memoir would sell as well as a book exclusively about punk bands would.

My friend and fellow record label/store owner, Bob Suren, had done well when he published his first book, Crate Digger: An Obsession with Punk Records with Microcosm. When his book reading tour passed through Tucson, Julianna and I were in the handful of people who attended. I had stayed in touch with Bob after his bookstore appearance, asking for advice, and I was hopeful that Microcosm would be my main distributor, so it was a disappointment when they pre-ordered only ten copies. I was also disappointed to hear that Last Gasp was no longer selling books that they didn't publish themselves since they had been my main book supplier back in the Toxic Ranch days and even further back to Pomona.

Those setbacks aside, I forged ahead, getting in touch with several record stores I had dealt with in the past and some new ones I found on social media, offering them direct wholesale pricing. Orders started to pick up and gained some steam when a few of those stores sold out the first batch and placed reorders for the book.

I had sent a book to Brad Bohonus, since he had contributed to the oral history, along with a couple of photos. He asked me why the book had no ISBN, a code that enabled libraries, wholesalers, and bookstores to manage inventory. Many retailers won't even sell a book without an ISBN on the barcode. Neither Matt at Fluke nor I knew about this when we sent it off to the printer. I always hated barcodes, but realized Brad was right. If I wanted to get the book in more places this was a necessary evil so I ordered ISBN stickers and put them on all the remaining books. I also got some good advice from Peter Davis from Your Flesh magazine as to who I should send the book to for reviews.

One day, I got a Facebook message from my old friend Kurt Ross (from the bands Red Brigade and Kent State) about a festival being planned in Pomona called New Values. It was to be a one-day event held at the old LA County Fairgrounds with tons of punk bands, such as Iggy Pop, the Misfits, Damned, Exploited, TSOL, Black Flag, Agent Orange, Cro Mags, Dickies, Social Distortion, Adolescents, Steve Ignorant of Crass, L7, Jesus Lizard and tons more on three stages. Jello Biafra would DJ the event.

I noticed the date it was taking place, June 8th, just a couple of months away. Since I knew Kurt had worked for Goldenvoice in the past, I asked him to see if they had any table space for vendors. How could I resist the opportunity? A huge punk festival in fucking Pomona, of all places, and I had just published a book about punk starting up in the Inland Empire, with the Pomona storefront on the cover. Now there was this festival in Pomona and to top it off, it was on my birthday!

Kurt made a couple of phone calls and he quickly got back to me. I was welcome to set up a table. Besides beer and food, there would be other vendors, like Vans, Dr. Strange Records, Dogtown Skates, and the Punk Rock Museum, with some vague talk about including murals at the festival to document the history of punk rock in Pomona. For now I had to get the permits to sell in California, including a City of Pomona tax license, something I hadn't needed since 1987.

I had Don Rock from Terror print up some Three Eyed Baby Toxic Shock shirts once I heard he had recently found the screens from the original design he did for me back in the 90's. He did a sizable batch of those and immediately I got an order in Japan for a large portion of the shirt run. I asked him to print more, but unfortunately he was just too busy travelling.

I set about doing my first public appearance to promote the book. Despite my introverted personality, I knew I had to overcome my shyness unless I wanted the 1500 books that filled up the back room of my house to start collecting dust. Record Store Day was coming up and it seemed that Wooden Tooth in Tucson would make sense for my book launch, as they were the current hip record shop that filled the void after Toxic Ranch closed up in 2014. They were located one block and down the alley from our old store. I got in touch with the owners and they said they would be happy to host me. They made a poster and asked former Toxic Ranch volunteer Shane Muldowney to be the DJ for the event.

I had been to only a handful of book signing events. The first one was in 1988 with social activist Ed Sanders, a member of both the Yippies and the experimental band the Fugs. He had written several books, including a bestseller about Charles Manson, The Family. He was signing a new book of his poetry at the Anaheim Convention Center. (I'm not sure I even finished that one.) I also met environmental activist Ed Abbey on two occasions before he died where his books were signed. Those I did finish.

I heard book events were sometimes accompanied with coffee and cookies, but I thought that sounded terribly cliche. As an alternative, I thought, why not a vegetable? I had always brought home leftover food from my weekly hotel job, as opposed to seeing it end up in the garbage, and one thing I had access to was an endless supply of broccoli. At Wooden Tooth, it turned out to be the perfect ice breaker, when people stumbled across my table of books and other Toxic Shock-related merch.

"Please help yourself to some broccoli", was my opening line and also my parting signature as they left the record store, with or without my book in hand. In the back of my mind, I thought even Julianna would approve, as in her later years we used to joke about opening a Toxic Ranch Vegetable Store every time we passed by a vacant storefront. Since our record shop spent its last twenty years in Tucson, there was a good turnout at Wooden Tooth. I was able to sell a decent amount of books and it was a fun time.

The next event was in Phoenix. We had purchased tickets to see Neil Young and Crazy Horse that evening, so Matt at Fluke helped me set up a book signing event at the long running indie store, Stinkweeds Records, that same afternoon, before the concert. It wasn't as well attended as the Wooden Tooth event, but the few that showed up were happy to get the book and the guys running the shop that day were nice and friendly. The broccoli made its second appearance and Neil and Crazy Horse were pretty damn great that night.

Other Neil and Crazy Horse tour dates were in Huntsville, Alabama, followed by Nashville. I'd never been to Huntsville, but I knew of the band Knockabouts, who were featured on 1983's Barricaded Suspects compilation. I tracked down an indie record store called Vertical Records, situated in Lowe Mill, an old textile factory that was converted into a mall of various alternative shops. The owner, Danny, was receptive to my idea of hosting my book tour and he knew how to get a hold of Donnie Sharp, the singer of Where's My Viet Nam by the Knockabouts. We flew into Nashville, spent the day exploring downtown and the Country Music Hall of Fame, and drove out to Leipers Fork, a quaint little town in rural Tennessee, with a novelty shop that sold Lord Phartwell's Whoopee cushions. I couldn't pass that up. The check-out clerk asked if I wanted it gift-wrapped, but I told her I was planning on using it immediately.

The next morning we stopped at a Buc-ee's, the legendary massive travel center on the way to Huntsville. Unfortunately among their thousands of offerings, Buc-ees didn't sell any broccoli. We did purchase some Beaver nuggets after visiting the world's cleanest bathrooms. With GPS and wandering on foot through the inside of the huge factory, we found Vertical Records and set up our table of books and t-shirts. Danny was very hospitable and it was great to finally meet Donnie, who was now in a band called the Go Go Killers. Beside Donnie, the only other person who dropped in was a friend of Fluke who heard about the event.

In Huntsville, it was hard to tell the church steeples from the numerous missiles on the horizon at the Space and Rocket Center. That night Neil and the Horse did an awesome set of tunes at the Orion Amphitheater, kicking it off with Cortez the Killer and ending up with Fucking Up as the encore. I was a tad disappointed that Southern Man wasn't included in the set, but the Alabamians really dug Neil. Surprisingly, there was no heckling and the security at the venue wasn't as uptight as in Arizona, so people weren't prohibited from dancing in the aisles.

The next morning we drove back up to Nashville, visiting Third Man Records, owned by Jack White. We left a book sample with the cashier working that day. We also checked out Grimey's, which is a great Nashville record shop with a music book store in the basement. In the weeks leading up to our visit, I hadn't been able to find any place to host a book stop in this city, but Grimey's was nice enough to take some books on consignment and hung up a promo poster for it. In nearby Franklin, we had Nashville Hot Chicken in a place called Hattie B's and left a book sample with Luna Records, a much smaller shop in another converted vintage industrial building made into a shopping mall, called The Factory at Franklin. Luna wasn't selling books, but they were pleasant enough when declining.

That night we drove out to the site of the next Crazy Horse show to find out it was cancelled due to impending tornado activity. They rescheduled the concert and were honoring tickets the following day, when we had planned on flying home. We decided to extend our stay in Nashville one more day and were glad we did.

I got in touch with Julianna's younger brother Dan, who was now living in Spring Hill near Franklin, and we dropped by for a visit. He had gone through a rough stretch, battling cancer, then the unexpected recent death of his other sister Mindi and to top it off, getting laid off from his job in Tennessee at Mitsubishi Motors, after relocating from California for the job opportunity here. His house had narrowly avoided a direct hit from the tornados the night before. In spite of all this, he maintained his quick sense of humor and we had a nice visit.

Crazy Horse was incredible that night, probably the best I'd ever seen. It was held in an old rock quarry, so the acoustics were great. We found our cheap seats in the outskirts of the venue, but were soon approached by an employee of the place who asked us if we wanted to upgrade for free. To our surprise, we got moved to seats much closer to the stage.

The set list that night was expanded to include some gems like Vampire Blues, Powderfinger, and Roll Another Number. The sound was incredibly loud and clear and the moon was shining down on the surrounding rock walls that surrounded us. The band was in top form and I think they wanted to show their appreciation for the crowd that opted to return this night, as opposed to getting a refund. Whatever the reason, we were treated to two encores, with Danger Bird and Don't Cry No Tears from Zuma, followed by the rousing version of Sedan Delivery. I'm so glad we experienced this as it wasn't long before this tour fell apart due to some band members' health issues and I doubt we'll ever get to see Crazy Horse on tour again.

Things on the Airbnb front slowed down quite a bit from April to the end of 2024. We had a bunch of travel planned ahead to promote the book and I just don't feel all that comfortable with strangers in my house when I'm not there. There had been a couple of times when guests left the house with their set of room keys dangling from the padlock on the gate, where any passerby could grab them.

The No Values festival was fast approaching and I thought it would be a good idea to resurrect a Toxic Shock title that has been out of print on vinyl since 1983, the compilation Barricaded Suspects, as a companion piece to the book. Dr. Strange had done a CD version back in 2002, but by 2024 he didn't have any stock left. I tried in vain to get Bill Plaster to make some more CDs, but he said the format was dead.

I worked with Pirates Press to get a batch of vinyl pressed, using the original cover artwork and including the twenty-page Brainstorm fanzine insert. The vinyl was pressed in the Czech Republic and as we crossed our fingers, it arrived just in the nick of time for the festival in Pomona, in a limited batch of 465 copies.

I had high hopes of selling most of them at No Values. I heard from Paul at Goldenvoice that they had sold 40,000 tickets to this event and were planning on printing a free fanzine to be given out to all the attendees. Each band playing the festival was given space in the magazine, plus I was interviewed by the editor of the zine, Matt Diehl, for it as well. I was told a similar number of 40,000 zines would be printed and distributed. I had the Three-eyed Baby shirts from Terror and I got to work getting some other t-shirts made. I had my friend Bruno print some Toxic Shock logo, Peace Corpse's Terror of Quincy, and Barricaded Suspects designs, all designed by my old penpal Pushead. I had an eight- foot-wide banner of the Toxic Shock logo made to promote the book and I also found a place that printed stickers fairly cheap and quick, so we had a decent amount of merch to sell, so much merch, that I had to rent a bigger vehicle, rather than drive my Toyota Yaris.

Bruno had just printed a second issue of his own fanzine, Reset, and Matt wanted to bring all his Fluke publications to sell. We planned to all meet up in Pomona on June 7th and we went to the fairgrounds to set up our merch table for the big event on the 8th.

That afternoon, I had an in-store book signing event at Dr. Strange Records as part of a live-streaming thing that he does every week. That went pretty well and I got to reconnect with Angie and Tracy from Peace Corpse, along with Kurt Ross and countless other figures from the "Badlands" of the Inland Empire. Directly after that, we headed over to Matt the Rat's house in Pomona, where he had a backyard BBQ planned for my early 69th birthday party. More familiar faces showed up, including Bill Chen, Nathan Wilson (who also was the DJ for the party), Bob Durkee, Farrell from Decry, Linda Kite and Jack (who drove in from Burbank with Jef Travis), Tim Zaal, Mick Rhodes, the skate legend Steve Alba, and so many more, several of whom were at Dr. Strange earlier.

I discovered this book tour thing was like traveling on a time machine, connecting with folks I hadn't seen in years, if not decades. None of these people were ones Matt "the Rat" Estel knew, and vice versa, as our personal connection predated the store, when the two of us drove from Pomona to Chinatown and Hollywood to catch our first punk shows in 1979-80. Even so, he was a great party host, with his brother Marty manning the grill, dining tables set up across the backyard, an assortment of liquor and cold beverages in ice chests, and a PA system rented for a live band. He wisely had porta-potties set up in the rear of his backyard, so people didn't need to go inside his house to urinate. His older brother Greg, entertained the guests in his own special way, telling tall tales of the early Pomona scene.

Fred Wright had a cover band doing some punk classics, with Kurt and Mick doing Radio Moscow by Kent State, Farrell doing Dead Boys Sonic Reducer and Steve Alba playing some surf guitar tunes. At one point, I was asked to sing on a cover of Horror Snores and then I was joined by Bob Durkee on guitar for a rendition of Hey Bob, What's Up?. It was fun, even if I couldn't remember all the words. (I actually tried to look up the lyrics for Horror Snores online, with no luck. The only thing I could find was only accessible to Amazon Prime members! My lack of status prevented me from accessing my own lyrics I wrote thirty-four years ago!)

Afterwards, Matt Estel surprised me with a birthday cake that he had ordered from a bakery with a full-color reproduction of the book cover done in frosting! It was a really cool time and probably the best birthday party that I can remember.

Sara and I spent the night at Matt Estel's house and Bruno crashed on his couch. Matt Fluke drove in from Anaheim to meet us the next morning, and we drove back to our booth at No Values early in the morning, before the festival attendees were allowed inside. Bruno was able to sneak in a knife, several beers, and even some mushrooms past security and it took us awhile to get our table display set up. Goldenvoice provided us with a tent and electricity and we brought our own tables and lights. The crowd started filing in and bands began to play at 11 am. One of the first to play were the Adolescents. Shortly after their set, I was happily surprised to see Wil Gerkin and his wife swing by our booth. Wil was a Toxic Ranch employee/manager from the early 90's, who I hadn't seen in almost thirty years. He told me Tony Reflex was wearing a Toxic Shock shirt onstage during the Adolescents set and he had given us a shout-out to the crowd. Not long afterwards, Tony himself dropped in to say hello. Since business was initially pretty slow, Bruno and Matt Fluke took off to catch the Cro Mags.

As the day wore on, Sara and I took short breaks to catch sets by the Dickies, Jesus Lizard, and L7. She was particularly fond of the Dickies' catchy songs and their zany stage antics. I was able to get Bob Durkee a pass inside and he hung out with us, just like in the old Pomona days, chatting with customers and reminiscing.

Sales were okay, but nothing like what I was expecting from a festival of this size. It seemed most people were too busy running between the three stages to catch the bands and never found the time to check out the vendor area, as it was tucked far away from the main entrance and the heavily trafficked area between the three stages. I think Matt was disappointed that Fluke wasn't selling as well as Bruno's Reset zine. Even one of the Dr. Strange people complained that they felt they were being ripped off by the booth placement, so it wasn't just my imagination.

While out looking for a toilet, I bumped into Ed Colver, smoking a cigarette behind the Trust Records booth, where he was to sign photographs. I could tell he was visibly upset. It had taken him several hours being stuck on the freeway before he could get to the festival site and he was understandably, in a foul mood. He told me he had always hated festivals.

Lines for food and beverages were very long, but foot traffic was light for the "vendor village". Ed wasn't the only one upset with the festival's organization. Plenty of people complained about parking and gridlock, causing them to miss several bands they came to see. It also turned out those 40,000 fanzines were nowhere to be found. They were discovered, piled high on giant pallets in the parking lot after the festival was over, basically ignored.

As it got dark, we were able to catch sets by the Viagra Boys and L7, who were both great. A mass of people exited one of the stages after the Exploited (whom I'm not a fan of) finished their set and headed to the big stage for the co-headliners and crowd pleasers Misfits, whom I also never cared for. We were lucky to catch Steve Ignorant do a great set of tunes from the Crass catalog. When it was still in Pomona, Toxic Shock was one of the first distributors to carry everything on the Crass label, from Crucifix and Rudimentary Peni to KUKL, all those awesome 7"s and Bullshit Detector compilation LPs. It was a treat for me to witness Crass songs I was familiar with only on vinyl finally done live on stage. Meanwhile, Bruno was able to catch a bit of Iggy Pop's set and when he got back from that, we all decided to beat the traffic and exit the festival with our little merch wagons back to the van, while the Misfits did their thing to the adoring masses.

Pomona has certainly come a long way from the days of our little punk shop(s) on Holt Ave. Before heading back to Tucson, we visited Disneyland and the next day stopped at Zoinks! Records in downtown Pomona. I spent an hour doing an interview with the owner, Robert, about my origins in the Inland Empire, which would be used for an upcoming podcast he was putting together. Good to see a small business like Zoinks! still going in downtown Pomona. I also revisited the locations of the three still standing Toxic Shock locations and the P.A.L. boxing gym where I had put on some punk shows.

At home, I left a copy of my book in each of the rooms we rented out. It was ignored by most Airbnb guests, but once in a while a guest would comment on it. It was interesting to have my book and my innkeeper duties cross over. One lady told me she wasn't into the punk history aspect of it, but was moved by the chapter intros that documented Julianna's stroke years. She could relate, as she had recently lost her spouse to cancer. Another guest, Jamie from Brooklyn, asked me if he could buy a copy and I told him of the upcoming plans to hopefully take the book tour to the east coast in December.

June 22nd was next in line for the book tour and this time we had something set up in one of the most respected record stores, Amoeba. Granted, it was in the slow summer season at one of their smaller locations, in Berkeley, but it still felt like something special to me. We had started our trip on the Sunset Limited from Tucson, which was severely delayed due to a top speed of 35 mph. It turned out that the train's engine car conked out and was now being towed by Union Pacific freight equipment. We arrived in Los Angeles too late for our connecting train.

We were put on a bus to Bakersfield at LA's Union Station that connected to the San Joaquin train to Emeryville where we were picked up at the station by Chris Shirley from one of the bands on the Toxic Shock roster, Jesus Chrysler. I last saw him IRL (in real life) in 2013 when the band took me by surprise and got back together after a twenty-year hiatus, to play a one-off gig during the closure of Toxic Ranch in Tucson after a twenty four year run.. He gave us a ride to our cat-sitting house in Berkeley (Deanna was out of town again) and asked about the broccoli connection. I filled him in on the secret on our short drive and I invited him to join me for the book signing event.

The next morning, we accidentally ran into Chris again, and we met his wife, Lizzie, and her two adorable daughters at a breakfast joint on College Avenue. Later in the afternoon, Sluggo, another from the Toxic Shock fraternity and the guitarist from Hullabaloo, picked us up at the house, after fulfilling my request to pick up some broccoli on the way. I realized the last time we saw each other was in 1989 when Hullabaloo played Club Congress in Tucson. I also filled him in on the secret origin of the broccoli mythology.

On the way to Amoeba on foot, as we schlepped our box of books and merch, we walked past People's Park, which was now blocked off by shipping containers with armed guards on duty. Times had changed since my days of hanging out along Telegraph Avenue as in the mid 1970's.. The symbol of resistance since 1969 was now officially history, as the land was cordoned off to build more student housing. I sure hope they keep the mural that serves as a landmark, documenting the story of the sacred space.

 We were greeted at Amoeba by the manager Ray, who directed us to the "green room", a small employee breakroom. Surrounded by cardboard boxes of record store backstock, we were offered complimentary beverages and snacks. I felt like a celebrity!

Chris showed up to join us on a lively roundtable (truth be told, it was rectangular) discussion, while book and shirt sales were handled by the front cashier of Amoeba. The three of us talked about our shared history, as folks gathered around the record bins. I started to notice familiar faces as the crowd grew larger, such as Tucson Toxic Ranch employee and ex-Fells member, Jeff Glave and David Ewers, our last Toxic Shock employee in Pomona. Mike LaVella of Gearhead even dropped in for a few minutes on his way to work. A friend of Chris, Gil Warquez taped the whole thing and we fielded questions from the audience, one about the band G-Whiz and even a couple concerning broccoli. Afterwards, Sluggo treated us to a spectacular lunch at Burmese Superstar, before we headed over the bridge to San Francisco. We caught the Fluke-sponsored art exhibit from the guy who did Noxeen comics and we ran into the one and only Winston Smith, the infamous graphic illustrator. Sluggo bought a signed and framed Dead Kennedys In God We Trust poster from the legend before we returned to the East Bay.

The next day, it was Chris' turn to cart us around, as an impromptu Uber driver. I instructed him to pick up some broccoli before we headed to our first of two book venues that day, which was at Long Haul Info Shop from 2 to 4 pm. This was a DIY fanzine library and live music venue. I was to be the "opening act" for a few local punk bands.

Here, I finally got to meet Deanna Ewers, who was responsible for sharing her house with us in Berkeley in exchange for cat-sitting the last few years. Also I reconnected with another former Toxic Shock Pomona employee, Janet Rogers. I found out she had worked for Amtrak for a number of years, as a bartender among other duties. Ray Lujan from the band Pariah was also there. My old band Peace Corpse had shared a stage with them once at Shamus O'Briens in El Monte, opening for the F.U.'s from Boston.

I guess the Long Haul people expected an actual book reading as evidenced by a live microphone that was set up, but I ended up just shooting the breeze at the merch table with the few people that arrived. Lizzy's girls took the opportunity to sing a couple of songs acapella. Since I had set up another gig that day in San Francisco at Thrillhouse Records, we had to take off before the bands were scheduled to play, so we loaded up in Chris's car, with Lizzie and the girls, for the drive into the city.

I had originally wanted to do this one on Saturday night after Amoeba, but when Matt at Fluke heard about that, he got all bent out of shape, thinking I would somehow draw away from his art gallery event. I guess he thought San Francisco wasn't big enough for the two of us. I reluctantly agreed to reschedule it for Sunday to appease him. We arrived at Thrillhouse on time, before 5 pm and asked the clerk at the (mostly) empty record store where he wanted us to set up. He pointed to the back of the store where I saw a wooden staircase that led downstairs. Looking down, all I could see were a couple of outdoor trash cans. Upon further investigation, I saw a lonely table in the empty cavernous basement space where Thrillhouse usually held their live music events. It seemed no one was there for my shenanigans. I felt a bit like Neil Hamburger.

The person who I was in touch with to set up the event wasn't even there, so I asked the clerk if we could just do it upstairs. It seemed like a better idea to be visible in case a random customer walked in. I didn't think anyone would bother looking downstairs.

Chris invited his friend Rudy Fernandez to the store. I found out he was the person the Clash wrote a song about (Rudy Can't Fail) and he regaled us with stories of the first time the Clash came to San Francisco. Very cool guy.

Other than that, it was a pretty low key event. We hung out with Jennifer Jennings from the Pomona days, and one other person wandered in who wasn't familiar with Toxic Shock at all but bought a t-shirt because he liked the design. We took a couple of photos with Chris and the broccoli and then went out for Mexican food before heading back to the East Bay.

We had a train to catch early in the morning to Santa Barbara, where we dropped our bags at the station, walked out on the pier, and ate some seafood while taking in the sunset. Then we hopped the train north for the short ride to the more budget-friendly town of Goleta where we spent the night at a Motel 6. We flew home from the Santa Barbara airport back to the lake of fire.

Our next book stop was on July 9th, once again in Phoenix. This one Matt Fluke set up at Zia, a popular indie record store chain, with several locations here, plus one in Tucson and another in Las Vegas. Sara and I drove up from Tucson with our books and merch, the broccoli in an ice chest. The manager was super-welcoming, got us some beverages, and had a table waiting with a display of my books, t-shirts and the Barricaded Suspects LPs.

Amoeba Records, Berkeley with Gil Warquez, Sluggo and Chris
Victoria BC at Supreme Echo Records with Jason Flower

The signing was scheduled from 2 to 4 pm and on a Phoenix afternoon, as you might imagine, the heat was unbearable outside. Matt showed up and we hung out waiting for an hour or so, hoping someone, anyone, would show up. I noticed a foul smell filling the air and soon realized it was the broccoli. I made a mental note about the cruciferous vegetable for the future, as it doesn't travel well in summer conditions. I apologized to the manager for the olfactory offense and the lackluster attendance. She was nice about it, all things considered.

As 4 pm was approaching and we were about to hang it up, two teenage girls approached our table. They asked what a book signing was, as they had never been to one. I told them I was fairly new to the concept as well, but I explained this was it. I gave them an overview of the book in hopes they might pick one up. They said they didn't have much money, but asked if I could autograph a couple of the stickers.

After that, we headed to our concert that evening, the reason we chose this date in the first place. The New Kids on the Block were playing Phoenix and since Sara had put up with my musical taste with everything from Negative Approach, Melt Banana, Star Crawler to Os Mutantes, I figured it was only fair to go with her to see one of her faves, the popular 90's singing act. Not my kinda music, but I'll admit they put on a high energy show, in spite of the over 100 degree weather even after sunset. Towards the end of their two-hour set, they told the crowd they would be back in Phoenix soon, but suggested next time they'd be better off at an indoor venue.

Saturday, July 13th was another Zia Records event, also from 2 to 4 pm, but this time in Tucson. This one was much better attended, as several Toxic Ranch customers that missed the Wooden Tooth book signing showed up and we had fresh locally sourced broccoli for them and the curiosity seekers. The ride home was much shorter too.

There was another Neil Young and Crazy Horse show scheduled for Vancouver coming up. We decided to get tickets for that, since Sara had never been to that part of Canada and I looked forward to checking it out again. We wanted to take the Cascades train north from Seattle because at some point, we wanted to experience all the Amtrak routes and this one was on our list.

A couple of weeks prior, we found out the Vancouver concert was cancelled but that didn't deter us from our trip. We had a book signing planned in Seattle at Singles Going Steady Records for July 21st. For this one, we had Bradly Petrovich design the poster and we were amazed at the result. Bruce Lee was made of solid broccoli and was renamed Brocco Lee.

We flew into Seatac Airport and took the commuter rail into the city. After grabbing some high-end farm-fresh broccoli at the Pike Place Market, we walked over to the record store where Seattle was now going to be officially broccolified!

Our two hour-hang at the record store was a blast! It was awesome to see Bill Tuck, John Husok, Janet Brown and her son Matt, Andy Nystrom, David Portnow, and others! Bill Tuck had lent his youthful energy and enthusiasm to Toxic Shock in the early 80's in Pomona and in much the same way, John Husok did the same a decade later at Toxic Ranch. Having them both in the same room made for a perfect photo op. Thanks go out to Byron and Rob for opening up the shop on a Sunday, a day which they were normally closed. I also scored a swell Feederz t-shirt at Singles Going Steady.

Early on Monday we boarded the Cascades at the beautifully renovated King Street Station for the three-and-a-half-hour ride to Vancouver. We had a stunning view of the Pacific Coast, especially Skagit Bay on the way to Bellingham. I also discovered the best damn cup of clam chowder of my life in the Cafe Car.

Going through Canadian customs at the Pacific Central Station was surprisingly quick and easy. Walking out from the station, we discovered two things. Our phone data plans didn't include coverage in Canada and also British Columbia has their fair share of Fentanyl zombies. We found a Tim Horton's shop to access Wi-Fi and get our bearings so we could get to our Airbnb out in suburban Burnaby, using the city's transit rail, the Sky Train. I fell in love with Tim Horton's brewed coffee, so much better than Dunkins or Starbucks.

Not unlike my first visit to Vancouver in 1980, I was trying my best to navigate by map and without the luxury of GPS. We were unable to even hail a Uber without cell service. Crazy how much we depend on these little devices, but these are first world problems. As an Airbnb superhost, I had earned a hundred dollar voucher from Airbnb and months earlier I used it to book a stay in Burnaby, near Deer Lake Park where the Neil Young concert was going to be. This suburban locale was our base for a couple of days as we explored Stanley Park, the Aquarium, and downtown Vancouver. We planned on taking a ferry to Victoria on the next day, which might have been more enjoyable, but Sara had caught food poisoning from some fish 'n chips in the city. The ferry itself was much nicer than we expected, featuring a full service cafeteria and other amenities that made the three-and-a half-hour trip go by quickly.

From the ferry landing, we took the local bus into Victoria, getting off to make an unannounced visit to Supreme Echo Music Boutique, Canada's smallest record store, (quite possibly the world's?), and its owner Jason Flower. The size of a small newsstand or broom closet, if more than two customers walked in, the third person would need to wait outside. I had bugged Jason for months with requests to host me for a book event, but he declined and now I could see why.

The place was packed floor to ceiling with rare, new and used records. I gave him the Decry t-shirt that Farrell had given me at the Pomona BBQ, as it was a size too small. I gently coerced him into trading two copies of Barricaded Suspects (featuring Victoria's own Red Tide) for a Dishrags LP and a couple of his books on the history of Victoria punk for mine. He had another customer waiting, so we had to split the scene, continuing on the bus to the city center, with all its British Empire inspired architecture and charm.

Sara wasn't feeling well at all unfortunately, but we explored the Miniature World, the renowned tourist attraction full of intricate dioramas as best we could, before heading back on a double decker bus to catch the ferry back to Vancouver, and home the next day. Not sure what it is with Victoria and miniatures, but we liked it! Another thing we noticed about Canadians is their polite manners. Just about each rider would verbally thank the driver as they exited the bus. I've never seen that happen in the States.

I was finding out that promoting a book about a record store is trickier than I thought. You'd think most record stores with any sort of interest in punk history would be open to the idea of having a book signing event for a book about record stores and the story of the people behind them. That's not always the case and few were willing to grant me a couple of hours in their shops. Maybe like the post office clerk once said, I am thinking that I'm too "all important." I kept plugging away, but many emails and messages tended to get ignored, especially in bigger "music" cities like Los Angeles, Vancouver, San Francisco, Chicago, Nashville, Minneapolis, Austin and New York.

After the Seattle stop took place, I noticed there was a little bit of interest on social media for me visiting Portland, Oregon. I had tried for weeks with no luck, but finally 2nd Avenue Records got back to me.

To confirm a date and time, I had to go through one of their former managers, Jay Martin who had since moved to Yucca Valley. I had met Jay at the Happy Universe gig in the high desert.

We wanted to take the Empire Builder from Portland to Spokane, a place I've been wanting to revisit, but this time with Sara. It just so happened that Ween, a band I've dug for decades, was playing Spokane as part of their 40th Anniversary tour. I got tickets for that and got in touch with a record store called Resurrection to secure a book gig with the owner, Mike.

It wasn't long before we hit the road again, flying into PDX and catching a ride with a Facebook acquaintance Steve Shook and his wife Alma from our airport area hotel to downtown. Naturally I had to ask them to score some broccoli for our stop at 2nd Avenue Records on August 3rd. It's good to have dealers of the green stuff willing to accommodate my unusual request.

It turned out to be a nice reception for my Books 'n Broccoli tour in Portland with some friendly faces. What made it special was that the people that showed up were mostly expats from both Tucson and Pomona. Chris Cilla, Dean Miles, and Mel Ford (from FUCT) represented Tucson and Ron Ranallo (Mad Parade) and Tommy Wilson repped the Inland Empire crew. Everyone seemed to enjoy the get-together and the broccoli. Steve was nice enough to drop us off at the train station and it was there I accidentally ran into Ike Becker, another FB friend, who just happens to work for Amtrak. Ike was also the very first person to buy my book online once I put it up for sale.

The train ride was quite scenic as it crossed the bridge to Washington State and hugged the Columbia River Gorge for many miles. We had taken this route one time before on our way from Seattle to Minneapolis, but with a delayed departure, it was dark so we missed out on the river views. This time we were lucky and we pulled into Spokane on schedule around midnight.

The next day we rented a car, drove to Resurrection Records and met Mike. There wasn't an area or table for displaying our merch, but we improvised by piling our stuff on top of one of his record bins. Somehow we overlooked picking up broccoli and perhaps it jinxed us for this event. Mike was super friendly and accommodating, but not a single soul showed up. He probably felt bad for us, so he bought two of everything we had brought with us, books, records, t-shirts, and stickers . Not to be discouraged, we celebrated our "success" by going out for schnitzel for dinner. Tucson has a million Mexican restaurants, but for German cuisine? Not a single one.

Before the Ween concert, we explored my old Spokane haunts from the '70's such as the urban waterfalls, the Halloween party house by the coffin factory, the apartment where I was arrested for selling mescaline on my nineteenth birthday and of course downtown. The Crescent department store where I had once worked as a janitor was now converted into offices.

We made our way along the river to the concert site. The stage was set up in an open air park, underneath the canopy that once housed the U.S. pavilion, on the site of the 1974 World's Fair. I was amazed how Ween had amassed such a huge following since their days on Shimmydisc Records. Folks had driven in from Montana, the site of their last show. It looked like their huge fan base were mostly connoisseurs of the "Jam band" music scene, a far cry from the handful of outsider music fans they had originally appealed to from their start forty years ago. I did catch them once in Tucson at the Rialto sometime in either 2001 or 2007, where I noticed their expanding audience, but this time it was wild to see this huge of a crowd in Spokane!

Ween delivered a two-and-half-hour set, including some gems like Pork roll egg and cheese, Touch my Tooter, With my own bare hands, Object, Devil's Dick, and Piss up a rope. As fate would have it, Spokane was the site of their very last live show as the band would cancel the rest of this tour and went on a "hiatus" due to Deen Ween's mental health. We were so lucky to experience this great night of music.

Sara's family now lives in Rochester, Minnesota and we like to pay them a visit whenever possible, so I figured for our next trip there, I'd explore some options in the area to promote the book. The ideal book tour trip would be to pack in three events during my five days off, giving us time for travel and a concert or other non-book related fun stuff. The Minnesota state fair was coming up and I knew Minneapolis had several good record stores so I reached out to a few without much success.

On Instagram, I discovered Rochester had a record store called Hidden World. I also realized Cedar Falls, Iowa wasn't terribly far away, only two hours south. I figured a visit with Barb Schilf and Dave Deibler-from House of Large Sizes in their hometown would be cool. Dave had expressed some interest in a book signing early on at his live music venue/bar called Octopus that he started in 2012 and I had always wanted to see Mohair Pear, a boutique that Barb had opened up in 1995.

Thursday, August 22nd was the first event. The weather was perfect and the owner of Hidden World, Vy, was really nice to us. It felt like a truly underground spot, tucked behind an alley with a green garden in the backyard. We mounted our "book sold here" banner on his fence and hung out while his regular customers began to fill in the small space, a two-room store loaded with new and used LPs. Very cool folks who knew about the Toxic Shock label seemed excited to pick up the book and some t-shirts, as Vy plied me with a couple of cans of a local beer. The owner of the brewery herself dropped by and bought a book at a friendly gathering which made the two hours fly by quickly.

The next day, we drove up to Minneapolis and had lunch at Kramarczuk Deli (famous for cabbage rolls since 1954!) with Jon Senum, formerly of Sonic Warp, who was a crucial promoter of punk shows in the area during the 80's and early '90's. A poster from one of his shows is in my book, a gig with three Toxic Shock bands (Hullabaloo, House of Large Sizes, and Jesus Chrysler) supporting the Cows. Legend has it, Hullabaloo blew the Cows off the stage that night.

After driving by Sara's old neighborhood and finding broccoli at the local grocery store, we found Extreme Noise, the all-volunteer run punk record store. We were greeted by Trisha Kaaos and set up our books and broccoli carnival act on top of one of their glass counters. It's a cool store, opened in 1994, that focuses on punk, hardcore and crust. Tons of vinyl, back patches, stickers, t-shirts and a decent selection of books. A bit like Dr. Strange, but without the bright colors and juvenile humor. This event was a bit better than Spokane. By that, I mean we had one person who dropped by to see us, Kacey Fisher, who brought his young daughter in for a signed copy of the book. The person who set up this gig, Phil, came by as we were wrapping it up and bought some books and merch from us to sell at the shop, so it wasn't a total loss.

The next morning, Saturday, we met up with Sara's family at the Minnesota State Fair and spent the warm summer day along with throngs of people, exploring the huge fairgrounds with its multitude of food offerings and exhibits.This one makes the LA County Fair in Pomona pale in comparison. You betcha!

On Sunday we drove down to Cedar Falls, a pleasant two-hour drive through cornfields and farmlands, marred only by the occasional Trump billboard. It was great to hang out and catch up with Dave Deibler at Octopus, setting up our merch at a table in front of the bar. We sold our last Three-eyed Baby shirt here. A few friendly Iowan folks dropped by and

I could see that Dave is truly a pillar of his community. Right next door is Mohair Pear, the shop run by Barb, who unfortunately was out of town, but I bought an Iowa t-shirt as a souvenir. Both people and businesses are Iowa institutions worth supporting. Visit them when you're in the Midwest and listen to House of Large Sizes! You can thank me later!

Most of September was spent back in Tucson. Since its release, I had dropped copies of my book on consignment at a number of local indie book stores, Antigone, and Bookmans. Since I heard they had a local author section, I even went to both Barnes and Noble locations in town. To my surprise, one day, when I was checking to see if any sales were made, the manager of Barnes and Noble asked me if I'd be interested in participating in a book signing featuring local Tucson authors. They had a number of dates open, usually on Sunday, so I said "Sure thing" and chose September 2nd. They had a table set up for me when we arrived, with my suitcase of goods and my token bowl of broccoli. My expectations were low, as we had already done two Tucson events and I figured local people were sick of hearing about my book. To my surprise, a few folks made it their destination that day, including Nick Gomez, Chris Carlone and Yousseph El Boujami, a success by my standards.

After much back and forth, I was finally able to convince a bookstore in Los Angeles to host a book event. We took the Sunset Limited, rented a car at the Burbank airport, and spent the day exploring the Lasky-DeMille Barn in Hollywood and the Westwood Village Memorial Park to visit celebrity gravesites. I also did a fun radio show with Stella Stray Pop at KXLU at some ungodly late/early morning hour. I have Linda Kite to thank for that, since they're old pals.

On the day of the gig, September 30th, we visited the La Brea Tar Pits and Forest Lawn Cemetery in Glendale. This book event was at Stories' Books and Cafe in Silver Lake. I had asked Ed Colver to join me, as he had

tland, OR - 2nd Ave Records with Ron of Mad Parade

Spokane WA with Mike at Resurrection Records

Minnesota State Fair, 2024

Rochester, MN - Levi welcomes us to Hidden World

Minneapolis MN Extreme Noise Records with Kacey Fisher and Stevie (photo by Trisha Kaaos)

Stories Books with Ed Colver,
Los Angeles, CA

Tucson, AZ - Barnes and Noble with Nick Gomez and F

kindly contributed several of his photographs to my book. He happily agreed to come along as a special guest. Luckily the store was a short drive from Ed's house in Highland Park, so we scooped him up and hit the 110, the oldest freeway in Los Angeles, with its tight curves and short on-ramps, while Ed told us stories of how he narrowly escaped numerous collisions on this freeway.

Once we arrived at the book store, Ed lit up the first of his endless supply of cigarettes and took up residence on the front sidewalk, as we met Art from Art's Building, a fixture from the art and music scene in the Pomona days. After sorting out where the book reading was to be held, I assured Ed that the outdoor patio in the back of the store wasn't designated as No Smoking, so he could safely mosey back there with his stogies, and we could get this thing rolling. Unlike Barnes and Noble, they had a little stage set up with a microphone and a few rows of folding chairs for whoever might show up. I basically let Ed do most of the talking and he entertained the assembled group with stories of early 80's punk events and characters. It was also great to finally meet Peter Davis in person, as he put out one of the first and longest running punk fanzines, Your Flesh. I've interacted with him many times over the decades, but never actually met him until now. I didn't bother with broccoli for this event, as I figured it wouldn't be necessary with Mr Colver's starpower. My favorite quote from Ed that night was " I got a bone to pick with vegetarians".

We took a couple weeks off from the road and finalized our plans for the next book jaunt. I wanted to do this one all by train, specifically three cities served by the Sunset Limited. We named it the Southern Discomfort Whistlestop tour. I had Brad Petrovich design posters for each individual event and Welly Artcore designed one for all three events on one poster, using the Barricaded Suspects artwork.

Our train pulled into San Antonio at 4 am on Friday. We had breakfast along the Riverwalk before visiting the Alamo and renting a car downtown, (ironically not from Alamo). The venue that night was Flagship Records, run by the charming couple Dano and Patrice, which is part of the Corn Pound complex owned by Jeff Smith of the Hickoids. We picked up some broccoli and cornbread at a local Hy-Vee supermarket on the way. If you need to ask why cornbread, you don't know the Hickoids.

Jeff greeted us at the record store and gave us a full tour of the Corn Pound. This was much more than a record store. It contained the office for High Voltage Music, a nonprofit organization/music school for at-risk teens, plus an office for the Saustex record label, a recording studio, a live music venue, and rehearsal space. Pretty damn impressive.

We set up our little merch circus on one of their display cases and Jeff introduced me to the mostly younger faces in attendance, describing how the punk/indie distribution network existed before the internet. On the wall behind us were displayed several Toxic Shock-related records, posters and ephemera that Flagship had put together prior to my arrival. I took some questions from the audience and just soaked up the friendly vibe of the place. Unbeknownst to me, in another room of the complex, Jeff had assembled half the band (Tom and Harvey) for an impromptu acoustic set of Hickoids songs, such as "Driftwood 40-23". Jeff traded me a Hickoids shirt for a Peace Corpse Quincy t-shirt. It turns out, we're both fans of Jack Klugman. It was an extra special and fun day.

Since the Sunset Limited truly is limited (running only three days per week) we needed the rental car for the three-hour drive to our next gig in Houston on Saturday.. But the drive wouldn't be complete without another visit at Buc-ee's travel stop extraordinaire. After using the world's cleanest restrooms, filling up our tank with gas and our stomachs with Beaver Nuggets, a caramel coated corn concoction, we hit the road, went into the humongous metropolis of Houston, found our way to Cactus Music, and met up with David Ensminger, the prolific book author and drummer who set up the day's festivities.

David was the very first person to give my book a review when it came out and really went the extra mile to make this a memorable afternoon. He arranged for a newspaper interview and a radio station plug ahead of the event. A stage is a fixture at Cactus, since they often do live in-store performances. To the side of the stage, the merch table was handled by Sara, as David and I talked about our books, including his newest, Austin Punk Invasion, and we did some Q and A. It went by pretty quickly, then Ty Gavin and Xavier from the Next did a set of tunes and told stories.

Both Ty and Xavier were quite personable and were as curious about my story as I was of theirs.The Next were one of the very first Texas punk bands and had at one point enlisted future Hickoids members Davy Jones and Richard and Arthur Hays in the band. May they all rest in peace. Along with another deceased Hickoid, Jukebox, they certainly left their mark.

It seemed half of the Houston punk scene was there, including Nikki from Verbal Abuse, JR Delgado from Doomsday Massacre, and Linda from the Mydolls. A former regular customer at Toxic Ranch, Ryan, was also there, as he had moved here from Tucson. It was also really nice to run into Shane Allbritton. It had been a long time. Shane was the art director/Svengali for the world-famous Otter Pops garage punk trio back in Tucson circa 1994-95. Her family also has deep roots here in Houston, with a chain of Allbrittons cafeterias that unfortunately are now gone and long shuttered.

The best part of a book tour is reconnecting with old friends. Afterwards, most of us all met up at Freebirds for burritos. Later that night, I got to meet Bob Weber, drummer of Really Red and Culturcide and head honcho of C.I.A. Records. We met at David's place, then went out for a drink at a local watering hole.

Back in 1980, when I started up Toxic Shock, C.I.A. Records was one of the first labels outside of California that I carried. I discovered them while leafing through a Slash magazine and saw their advert. The Really Red 7"s were amazing, the Teaching You the Fear LP was even better, and then it was the MyDolls and especially Culturcide that blew my mind. I was lucky enough to see both Really Red and Culturcide live, when they finally toured L.A., in 1983 and 1985 respectively. Just amazing stuff to witness!
It was really great to chat with Bob after all these years and he gave me a couple current C.I.A. titles, the Manifestation compilation CDs, which I've been listening to in my car. I also was given a cool little book David wrote about Axis prisoner of war camps in the States during WWII called Enemies in the Backyard.

The next morning, David took us out to the House of Pies and then to Glenwood Cemetery where Howard Hughes is buried, before dropping us off at the Amtrak station for our continuing nine-hour journey to the Sunset Limited's terminus, New Orleans.

We had a room booked with my employee discount at a newer Hilton property, which had a retro 1940's theme going on with its decor, adjacent to the World War II Museum. We spent the morning walking about the French Quarter, then went off to the Bywater neighborhood for our book event at Euclid Records, owned by Lefty Parker. Back in 1985-86, Toxic Shock had a distribution center in this city and even had a retail record store at 333 Burgundy, which is now a wedding chapel.

Sara and I love this city. This was the third time we'd been here in the last three years. Euclid Records was the place to be on a lovely Monday evening, although there was a sparse turnout for this one. Most of the people I knew in the punk scene here had passed away or moved elsewhere, it seems.

After we set up our table, we met Pat Roig and enjoyed thumbing through his book From Stapleguns to Thumbtacks New Orleans Flyer Art 1982-1995, which led to amazing stories of punk lore from both Pat and Chris Fronseca of the band Shell Shock. It seemed each page had an accompanying oral story and it's a thick book! It was both historic and hysterical! From here, we flew to Phoenix to catch a rescheduled Electric Light Orchestra concert, which was pretty great. Then we headed home.

Most of November was spent back in Tucson. It was finally cool enough weatherwise to enjoy life in the desert. Of course, the presidential election results came in and our hearts sunk, knowing we'd be dealing with Trump in the White House yet again. We had one odd Airbnb guest, a goofy young dude who was getting a bunch of tattoos done and needed a place to chill in between sessions. We got a message from him one day that said he wanted to warn us that a feral cat was on the loose in the yard. He said it had jumped on his lap and sneezed blood all over him. We had to explain that it was our toothless black cat Larry, who we had rescued from the Pima Animal Shelter and that he was not feral. He is the sweetest natured cat and was probably just looking for affection when he jumped into Tattoo Man's lap.

Also, at my Hilton job, we got some regular guests frequenting the social hour. The typical guest here would stay for 30 days, sometimes longer. We would get people waiting on insurance claims for home fires and floods, and even some Dutch Air Force personnel sent to Tucson's

Davis Monthan Air Force base for training. One of those who regularly enjoyed the free glasses of Dos Equis was a Border Patrol agent from Texas. We started talking about music, once he found out that I had a background as a record store owner. As I got to know him better, I found out he was actually in charge of Internal Affairs for the Tucson sector. I could tell, as time went by, he was growing weary of his job, bemoaning the direction that his agency was now taking. It was now expanding and looking at property for air transport of deportees and land to be purchased for concentration camps. He would dryly joke as he compared all this to the history of Nazi Germany. They were already discussing plans for the near future under a new administration. I could tell he wasn't looking forward to the rapid expansion and was certainly looking forward to retirement.

Also in November, an in-depth interview I did in the summer with Welly Artcore came out in his Artcore fanzine and my pal Sluggo self-published his book Gutargonaut. November 8th 2024 was our third Anniversary of living together, so I took Sara out to the Silver Saddle Steakhouse and then took a nice drive to Green Valley to see the Titan Missile Museum. After all, nothing says love like a decommissioned ICBM. Seriously, the day Sara decided to move to Tucson and be my partner in life was a great day indeed. She was my lifesaver in a time when both of our lives desperately needed companionship and more importantly, love.

December we had saved for a couple of biggies on the book tour, New York City and Washington DC. However, before we tackled that, we flew into Toronto and hopped a bus to go see the Canadian side of Niagara Falls. I've been wanting to see this for some time, ever since my older sister Curl told me how spectacular it was when she saw it in person. Scratch this one off the bucket list. Like the Grand Canyon, the photos really don't do it justice. Such an amazing vista and surreal experience it is to actually be there. I was glad we did it in winter to avoid the crowds.

San Antonio, TX - Flagship: Patrice, Jeff, Sara, me, Dano)

Houston, TX - Cactus Music with JR Delgado and David Ensminger

New York City NY-Times Square with my new pals (photo by Minnie Mouse)

Arlington, VA - Ian MacKaye at Dischord House

Quimby's, Brooklyn, NY:
Pamela & Gracie (Front) (Aaron C,
Steve S., Dakota & Jamie (L-R Back)

We took Amtrak's Maple Leaf on the border, which started out fairly empty, creaking along over an old rusty bridge. We disembarked for a quick customs inspection and continued down New York State along the Hudson River Valley, picking up more riders along the way. By the time we got to Penn Station, the train was packed.

Our hotel, the Distrikt, was a short cab ride away. It was one of those "boutique" hotels where Hilton took over a property, splashed some new colors on the walls, and renovated the tiny rooms. It was the only room with an employee rate, so I wasn't picky. It was near Times Square, which is where we walked the next day, in the brisk winter air. Before taking this trip, I had picked up a fluffy broccoli crown hat on eBay and was saving it for New York City. We ducked into a shop and I put it on. I found it was practical headgear in winter weather as it kept my ears warm. Nobody paid me much attention until we ran into a bunch of characters dressed in ridiculous costumes. Before I knew it, I was completely surrounded by two Spidermen, a Grinch, Minnie Mouse, and a tall, blue Statue of Liberty. They posed with us for a few photos and the Liberty guy even let me borrow his torch. For a minute, I felt the camaraderie as a bonafide member of a gang of Times Square hucksters.

That was short-lived though, as Minnie Mouse turned out to be a real bitch. She took Sara's phone and held it for ransom, telling us we wouldn't get it back unless we paid her a tip on a QR Code. After deciding we weren't giving in to her demands, we finally wrested it out of her hands.

We walked into a Hersey's Chocolate World where a couple of employees complimented me on my headgear and asked what I was promoting. I told them I was on a book tour around the country. They asked if it was about broccoli. To add to the confusion, my reply was "Not at all".

Sara wanted to have lunch at Tom's Restaurant, as many Seinfeld's episodes were shot there as Monk's Cafe. They had good soup. From there we took the subway to see the infamous Dakota Building, where Rosemary's Baby was filmed and John Lennon was shot. We moseyed over to Central Park, passed by the Strawberry Fields Memorial and over to the Alice in Wonderland statue on the other side by 5th Avenue. I had never been to the statue but recalled seeing it as part of the gatefold of the cover of Jimi Hendrix's Electric Ladyland album, so that made it special. I was also quite the spectacle evidently for some jaded New Yorkers, as they commented that they had never seen someone with a broccoli afro before. A couple of people even asked me to participate in their "selfie" ritual.

I had invited my old friend Steve Morris and his wife Pamela to our book signing event at Quimby's in Brooklyn. They live in upstate New York, so I was happy to hear that they were planning on making it to the city by bus. I hadn't seen him in real life since the late '80s, or the 1880s as I now like to call them. We met up at the insanely crowded Rockefeller Center and walked over to Bloomingdale's, since Pam wanted to do some shopping. From there, we took the subway over to Brooklyn. Luckily, as we were starving, we had enough time for really good pizza a couple of blocks from Quimby's before the book event.

The owner Steve Svymbersky at the book store was very gracious and had some kind praise for my book. His son was manning the register and his sweet shop cat Gracie was just the cutest. His shop was in a very narrow space, but packed with all sorts of reading material not found in your typical Barnes and Noble. We set up our stuff on a narrow table which Gracie promptly planted her furry body on. A trickle of people showed up, including a former Tucson record store customer, Dakota Pollock, who was a Charles Schmidt fan hoping to get a Pied Piper t-shirt. Jamie, one of our Airbnb guests who had rented a room from us awhile back also made an appearance and hung out. We had kept in touch via social media since his stay in Tucson. Aaron Cometbus, another author whose fanzines/books we had carried at Toxic Ranch also showed up for this one.

Steve Morris got into his Howard Cosell persona and started the thing off with some interview silliness. Aaron asked me to read something from the book, so I obliged and read a portion of chapter 5, recalling how Steve and I met through our mutual Yippie background and organized a Rock Against Racism concert in Los Angeles in October of 1979. At Quimby's, we picked up our souvenir from the Big Apple, the Abandoned Mattresses 2025 Calendar.

Speaking of Yippies, Aron Kay, "the Pieman," was calling each of us repeatedly during the day, asking us to visit him while we were in town. He was living in an assisted living facility a couple miles away and I had invited him to the book store. We had been on our feet all day long and had early travel plans in the morning, so we decided we needed to head back to our hotels in Manhattan to get some rest.

Steve and Pamela joined us for breakfast at our hotel, and to my surprise, had a gift for me. He had kept a canvas banner that I had made for the 1979 Rock Against Racism event in Los Angeles. It was huge, three feet high and at least fifteen feet long. "Smash the Nazis-Slam the Klan" it read. I had forgotten all about it until now.

We split up, as they had a bus to catch at Port Authority and we had a train to catch, the Northeast Regional to Washington DC. It was very packed with students and other people traveling for the upcoming holiday. Arriving at DCs Union Station, we quickly sorted out the local commuter line, Metrorail, to reach our hotel in Chinatown.

We had a three-day stay for this one. We spent the first two days exploring several Smithsonian museums and we walked along the Potomac river to the National Mall, all the way to the crowded Lincoln Memorial. I was particularly enamored with the FDR Memorial but the Korean and Vietnam Veterans Memorials were both impressive as well. However, being late December, although it was sunny, it was also really cold, at least for us desert rats.

Smash! Records was the site for our next book event, the last one for 2024. which took place on Sunday, December 22nd. I had a long history with this particular record store, as we used to distribute records to them back in the "1880s" when it was owned by Bobby in Georgetown. More recently, Matt Moffat was the owner, in a new location and we had also done some business there in more recent years. Matt was an early supporter of the book and we had sold copies to him directly.

Other than Moffat, the only person I really knew in DC was Ian MacKaye of Fugazi and Dischord Records.. While at the House of Pies in Houston, David Ensminger suggested that I should get in touch with him and gave me his email. I hadn't seen or been in touch with Ian since Fugazi came to Tucson for a gig at the Rialto on April 10th, 2001. Since Minor Threat, Dischord and Fugazi are featured in my book, I had sent Ian a copy of my book. He was kind enough to send a postcard to thank me for the gesture. I thought it would be ideal to get Ian as a moderator for this one, but he politely declined and that was understandable. He is a busy guy, running Dischord after all and he mentioned that he had only glanced through my book since receiving it. I asked him if it would be possible to at least visit the Dischord House during our visit. He said he would get back to me.

It was the 40th anniversary of Smash! as a record store, so to draw more people, Matt had the idea of having the band Bed Maker play an in-store set as part of the evening's festivities. Bed Maker had just released a new album that came out on Dischord. I found out that their singer, Amanda, had once worked at both Smash Records and Dischord simultaneously , so she was familiar with Toxic Shock. She had been the one boxing up our orders we placed with Dischord and who sometimes also placed orders from us for Smash. It turned out that Amanda is also Ian's younger sister.

On the night of the event, I was pleased to see a good size turnout for a Sunday evening at the record store. I wasn't too surprised, I figured Bed Maker had a decent following being a popular local band and that most people showed up to see them play rather than witness my awkward little book signing. Regardless, Matt and his crew were super nice to us. We found room to hang up our "Toxic Shock book sold here" banner behind the counter where we spread out our usual merchandise.

Like in New York, we hadn't found a store or bodega in DC where we could score some broccoli for this one, so gimmicks were a bit lacking. I didn't even bring my broccoli hat. As the band set up their gear, more people crammed the aisles between record bins and Amanda came up to the counter and introduced herself. Before I knew it, I was handed a live microphone.

I told the assembled crowd that I had written a book about record store life and congratulated Smash on their forty years of operation. Knowing I had more time to fill, I decided to read a chapter from my book. I think it might have been a part from chapter 4, since it covered the history of my first DC visit to attend the July 4th Smoke In in 1978.

I asked if anyone had read my book yet and I heard someone say yes. He then piped in about how the Yippies differed from your basic hippie and when I looked up I realized it was Ian. He gave some recollections of the early DC punk shows, when DOA did their first tour just a few blocks from Smash, at Madam's Organ, a Yippie-affilated living space that was also the site of some of the earliest Bad Brains and Teen Idles shows. Matt then commented on the punk rock and ice cream connection, as both Ian and Henry Rollins had once worked at Haagen Dazs while I was selling frozen confections out of an ice cream truck in Orange County during the same period in the late 70s.

I took a few more questions, one asking if I had any dirt on anyone in the punk scene. I told them they'd need to buy the book if they wanted the scoop on Rozz of Christian Death, recalling how John Waters was once asked why he didn't do podcasts. His reply was "I'm not giving it away for free." I concluded my book spiel and when it was over, I was shocked to get a standing ovation. The lack of any available chairs probably helped.

Bed Maker were up next and they quickly launched into their set of frenetic tunes, performing between the posters and the used clothes rack. It was a great time. Ian sauntered up after Bed Maker was finished and we chatted a bit. I thanked him for coming and he said he rode his bicycle down since he lived in the neighborhood, which explained the neon safety vest he was wearing. He said we should drop by the Dischord House the next day at 11 am. He would be unloading a large shipment of records in the morning, but he should be done by then. I did sell some books and people seemed happy to be there .I thanked Matt for the hospitality and we split with smiles on our mugs. It was good to end the book tour of 2024 on a high note.

After breakfast on Monday, we dialed up an Uber for the ride to Dischord House. We had the correct street address, but unfortunately, I didn't notice when I confirmed the ride that it was targeted for DC, not Arlington, Virginia.

When we arrived, I didn't recognize the famous porch where so much punk history took place and I texted Ian asking for directions. That's when I realized we had the right address but the wrong city. We had driven five miles in the wrong direction! The driver was kind enough to edit the ride and off we went on our way. As we entered Arlington, Ian called to see if we were still lost. I told him we had just passed the Iwo Jima statue and he said we were five minutes away.

This time I recognized the landmark and its distinctive porch, across the street from a nondescript commercial building. We rang the bell and Ian greeted us at the door, asking if we wanted to see the Dischord warehouse first. It turned out it was housed in the structure across the street. It had been a stained-glass repair and then a TV repair shop when Ian, Jeff Nelson, and the other Dischord people first moved into the house and Ian mentioned how they waited over a decade for the space to become available to rent.

As the Dischord label expanded over decades, it had outgrown the original iconic house and needed more room. Inside the warehouse were rows of neatly organized cardboard boxes containing all the label's inventory of LPs and CDs, plus separate offices for accounting, mail-order and a handful of employees. It reminded me a bit of the Rough Trade office in San Francisco when I met Ruth Schwartz in 1983.

Scattered about were plenty of photographs, artwork, knick knacks, and curios, including a miniature Ian MacKaye doll (complete with guitar and knitted cap) that was gifted to him by a fan. We then entered the iconic house and first thing, we went down to the basement where everyone from Teen Idles, Minor Threat to Fugazi would practice. It had a very low ceiling, which made it a challenge to avoid bumping your head, but if you wedged yourself in between the crossbeams you were able to stand up straight. Ian said the acoustics were great in the small tight space and fairly soundproof, to keep from annoying the neighbors.

My favorite part of the basement tour was watching Ian demonstrate how a small, used, beat-up clothes dryer, held together by copious amounts of duct tape, worked. It plugged into a standard 110 volt outlet. Fugazi loaded it into their van and took this thing everywhere on tour to handle all their laundry needs. He explained that on the road you usually had access to a sink, detergent and water, but a dryer was harder to locate so this one came in handy. Instead of wasting time at a laundromat, they could plug it in anywhere on the road. No more stinky, sweaty clothes.

Ian has amassed quite an impressive archive over the years. He played a song off a computer hard drive of a Bad Brains track covering a Wire song, an unreleased version of Waiting Room and some live audio from when Fugazi played Pomona in 1988. He even had a photo of that particular gig, where I saw the back of my head in the crowd, male-pattern baldness and all. He also had a funny story of their first tour stop in Spokane, when he invited the entire crowd on stage, to embarrass a couple of extra-rowdy slam dancers. The knuckleheads had been defending their aggressive activity, claiming it was part of the punk rock ritual. Ian asked them who made up these rules and he got their sincere reply, "Johnny Rotten."

Ian surprised me with a little something from my book. He still had the two bootleg CDs, the Kinks and AC/DC, that he bought from me during his Toxic Ranch visit on April 10, 2001. He told us the story of how the Smithsonian and the Library of Congress had expressed interest in acquiring the collection of artifacts and he declined their offer, explaining that the house itself was part of the history. Overall, I was quite impressed with the sheer volume of DC punk history that was meticulously organized and cataloged here, using his own money and the help of others with time and ability. I could only imagine the amount of work involved. I was taken aback by how generous Ian was with his time to show us around the place, but then again, he's always been a good egg.

Ian also has an extensive collection of Dischord correspondence, including letters he received from Toxic Shock during our expansion into New Orleans. He even had a postcard from a 15-year-old Dave Grohl, who was looking to form a band, stating he played guitar and knew some songs from Faith, Naked Raygun, the Headcleaners and Peace Corpse!

We wrapped up the tour by taking a few photos on the porch. I explained to Ian all about the books 'n' broccoli concept and how I had made some new friends in Times Square. I think he understood or at least found it vaguely amusing.

From Dischord House, we went to nearby Arlington National Cemetery to visit the JFK memorial. Later that evening, we checked out the MLK Public Library before heading back to our hotel for our last night in Chinatown. In spite of the frigid weather, I really love this city. Too bad Trump's going to stink it up for the next four years.

As 2024 came to a close, I was down to my last box of books and figured that was it, thinking there wasn't enough demand to reprint it. I thought an e-book edition would be cool for those people who prefer to stare at their devices rather than pick up an actual book of paper pages. Better than letting it disappear all together, I reasoned. I proposed the idea to Matt at Fluke and he said he really wasn't interested in e-books.

This is where Welly Artcore comes in. Being impressed with his Artcore fanzine and learning he published a couple of books himself, I asked Welly if he knew how to design an e-book.

I asked Matt to send me the files he had of the book, so we could move forward. I was surprised to get his response, which was basically "What's in it for me?" I had paid for everything myself on the Fluke edition. I had already paid him handsomely for his work in creating the layout. He always logged in every hour he put into it and I always promptly paid him for his time. Now he wanted more? His help with distribution was great, of course, getting my book into places I may not have been able to do myself, but for him to imply ownership of my work was beyond frustrating. It was disheartening.

Before I knew it, David Gamage at Earth Island in the U.K. got in touch with me expressing an interest not only in an e-book, but a second edition of the printed version. I was ecstatic to know someone was actually interested in financing a reprint and I approached Welly with this bit of news.

I had the written text, the bare bones of the book, on my laptop, but the edited version files with all the graphics were in Matt's hands. Welly had a deep background in graphic art, he actually went to school for it decades ago, prior to the digital takeover of publishing. He has made a lifelong career of it and is very familiar with the process of putting ideas to paper.

Fortunately, I had all the original photos and other artwork that was in the book. Welly was willing to start from scratch with fresh scans and said that to do justice to the book, it would be worth it in the long run. I sent him all the physical photos and other original artwork and he quickly got to work on redesigning the new layout. Within a couple of months or so, he was done.

Not only did it take far less time to complete than the first edition, but my pre-production cost was probably a fifth of what I had paid Matt at Fluke. Welly didn't charge by the hour or even ask for compensation really, but I paid him what I thought was fair for his time and skills. David at Earth Island was happy with the results, as it was practically a brand new book. What had taken myself and Matt at Fluke six months to compile was now expanded from less than 200 tiny pocketbook pages in its original limited U.S. release of 1500 to a 6" x 9" 338-page full-color work. Images that were originally the size of postage stamps now encompass half or full pages from brand-new scans. When I got my first batch of the new, improved books, I was very pleased with the results.

I had just finished reading the excellent self-published book GUITARGONAUT by Sluggo Cawley. I've known Sluggo since 1988, when Toxic Shock first moved to Tucson and we began talks to release an album from his band Hullabaloo, based in the Boston area.

The late 80's were an interesting time for punk rock. Major labels were just beginning to sign bands and soon ruin it for the underground. Sluggo has a knack for story telling and remembering all the small details of that time. The pages of his book are filled with malcontents, losers, drunkards, fuck-ups, and rag tag musicians. It tells about a time when a sense of community existed between like-minded, near-starving bands such as Skin Yard, SNFU, Hullabaloo,the Cows, the Hickoids and yes, Nirvana. Through Toxic Shock, I was glad to be able to connect Sluggo with Daniel House, Jack Endino, and Jeff Smith who've since become his best of friends for decades. I enjoyed reading about his encounters with other Toxic Shock label alumni like House of Large Sizes and Jesus Chrysler and got a chuckle from hearing his opinion of the Datura Seeds. Alt-Country/pop success? Ha! Another cool tidbit was when Sonic Youth were considering asking the Hickoids to be their support act for an upcoming major tour, but they opted for Nirvana instead. Imagine how that might've turned out! I introduced Sluggo to David at Earth Island, who agreed to have his book reprinted in the UK.

In March, Sluggo was planning a final show in San Francisco with his band the Grannies, after a long twenty-year run. I'd never had the chance to see his current band, so Sara and I planned a train trip for my first (and their last) show.The Grannies, like the Hickoids, aren't afraid to wear a dress and they take it a step further by performing as elderly ladies. Their final show was on March 29th at the renowned underground club Bottom of the Hill in San Francisco. It was also a celebration of his book release of GUITARGONAUT and since we shared the same publisher, Earth Island, I planned to bring copies of my book, Toxic Shock Assassin of Mediocrity, in its new expanded edition.

Sara and I took the Sunset Limited from Tucson to LA. The train actually arrived ahead of schedule. Since we had won a bid-up for a sleeper, they had a table waiting for us in the dining car. Yes, we shared a table with strangers and it wasn't all that awkward. I enjoyed a glass of red wine with my flat iron steak, which was tender and delicious. After dinner, I took a hot shower before retiring in the upper bunk of our roomette. I won't say I slept well, but I was able to get some sleep. (To all the whiners on the internet who complain of Amtrak's poor service, I'm sorry to report the bathrooms were clean and well-stocked.)

When I woke up, I realized we were already passing Pomona and our destination was next in line. Again, the train was ahead of schedule! On arrival at Union Station, we were able to use the Metropolitan Lounge for fresh coffee and complimentary snacks while we waited for our connection up the coast on the Pacific Surfliner.

The whole experience made airline travel pale in comparison. Sure, it's not the quickest way to get from one point to another, but at least it's civilized. In San Luis Obispo, we connected to an Amtrak bus that took us into the city of San Francisco. It was the first time with this odd connection, but if we had done the Coast Starlight as we had in the past, we would have ended up across the bay at a later hour in Emeryville. This way we arrived in the city, not far from our hotel on Market Street.

The next night was the show and it was so much fun! The Grannies knew how important it is to have a sloppy good time. They played as if it was their final performance, because it was. I loved hearing all their originals and the Devo and Wipers covers and now I see why the Grannies have had so many adoring fans since 1999. Sara and I helped sell plenty of their merch for them while they rocked the stage. After their set, we met Sluggo's wife Laurian while he signed copies of Guitargonaut and basked in the glory of performing one last time in front of many of his friends. I even sold one of my books to their singer, Dean.

The next two days were spent sightseeing, including trips to Fisherman's Wharf and the Cable Car Museum. I never realized until now that the SF cable cars are pulled by an endless loop of underground cables running a consistent nine miles per hour. For the car to move, it has to clamp onto the moving underground cable with a giant set of pliers! Who knew?

We also went to Chinatown for lunch and to an unbelievable stroke of good fortune, stumbled into the legendary Vale from Re/Search fame. For decades, I had read and admired so many of his works, including the Search and Destroy fanzine and books such as Pranks, the Industrial Culture Handbook, Incredibly Strange Music, Freaks, Angry Women, Modern Pagans and Incredibly Strange Films. We proudly sold these at my record store and through mail order. Today he was manning a garage sale of his many publications in the side alley called Jack Kerouac, next to the City Lights bookstore. After poking around the historic bookstore, where I dropped off a sample of my new book, I chatted a bit with Vale, telling him that, in my view, he was a true legend in the industry.

Shortly after our trip to San Francisco, sadly, we had to attend a family funeral. My sister's ex-husband, my brother-in-law, Henry DelCastillo had recently passed away after a brief but aggressive bout with cancer. The entire DelCastillo clan was there, gathering to honor the legacy of

"El Patron". He was a good man, a fantastic, loving parent to his eight incredibly gifted and lucky children. He excelled in business accounting and climbed corporate ladders at a time when Mexican Americans were pretty rare in that field.. Incidentally, he was one of the few Republicans I ever respected and looked up to.

I'm so glad to have reconnected with him in recent years. We had our widower status in common, as he had recently lost his second wife. He expressed his happiness that I had found a new love in Sara.

Shortly after Henry's memorial, the Del Castillos had to deal with yet another incredibly sad situation. Dan was still in the rehab hospital with his brain injury and was not getting any better. Five years had gone by, but his life was now reduced to staring at the wall and being fed by tubes. As a family, they decided it was best to end the prolonged misery and "pull the plug". This took place just two weeks after Henry's funeral.

On our way home, we spent two nights in Phoenix. Months ago, we had bought tickets to two completely different shows. First we saw the Melvins supporting Napalm Death at the Van Buren and the next night, we went to an incredible show that Kraftwerk put on at the historic, beautifully restored Orpheum theater.

Since my new book edition had an international publisher, I thought it was high time we crossed some borders to promote it. Both Sara and I had always wanted to visit Montreal, as we had heard it was the poor man's Paris. We also had a few more Amtrak routes to cross off our list. So we flew into New York City for one night's stay, arose early for a walk to Penn Station, then went traveling in style on the mighty Adirondack headed north, hugging the Hudson River. We boarded the long-ass train, with its multiple, almost empty cars that were so ancient they still had ashtrays built into the armrests.. We couldn't make out a single word of the on-board garbled feedback-laced public announcements.

Pomona CA June 2025 chopping it up with Bob Durkee during Justice League reunion show
(from a photo by Marhea Mc)
TOXIC
SHOCK
BARRICADED SUSPECTS
LIGHTS BOOKS
City Lights Bookstore
San Francisco
BOOKS
NOT
BOMBS
CONDOR
ntreal, Quebec - Sonik with Sara slinging swag
San Francisco - Vale at City Lights

We stopped in Albany (the home of Amtrak's headquarters) for an undetermined amount of time to divide the train into two shorter trains. My kind of travel, slow but steady! Once we crossed the border, a few Canadian Border agents came onboard the train to clear us through customs, which was far easier than I expected.

My very first international book signing event was held in Montreal, Canada on Saturday, May 3rd, between 2 and 4 pm, at Sonik Records. Earth Island had shipped them a box of books from the UK ahead of the event. This was also the 25th Anniversary of Sonik, THE punk record store of Montreal and they had a big punk show planned that night to celebrate!

I knew it was going to be good from the moment our Uber pulled up to the humble brick storefront where we were met at the curb by the gracious owner, Mathieu. Once we settled into our designated spot by the cash register, Mathieu brought out the broccoli charcuterie, complete with delicious hummus for dipping. If that wasn't enough, he brought out one chilled bottle of wine after another.

The people were so friendly and charming. We even met a couple Tucson expats, now living in Montreal. We sold several t-shirts and records. We actually ran out of books and wished we had brought more with us. After the event, we walked with Mathieu and his friends to an Italian restaurant for a pre-show dinner. The hospitality, the wine, the food, and the camaraderie amazed us. It was definitely a book tour highlight and simply a perfect day.

Montreal is a beautiful old world city. La meilleure séance de dédicaces de Toxic Shock à ce jour ! Montréal, c'est tout simplement génial ! Vive la Musique Sonik! In other words, congratulations to Sonik Records for operating a brick 'n mortar for twenty-five years.

We took Rail Canada to visit Quebec City the next day and while we were there, we dropped off some books and vinyl at Le Knockout Records, another cool little shop. Vive le punk! Vive le vinyl! Vive le Canada! Both Quebec and Montreal are beautiful cities steeped in history.

When we returned to Tucson, we had another invite from Barnes and Noble. This was on May 17th and was the local debut of the Earth Island edition. I like to call it the AARP version, due to the bigger text and enlarged photos. I also had some copies for sale of my new 28-page zine from Fluke, called Room for Rent. It was a fun low-key couple of hours, the highlight was when local recording studio owner Jim Waters dropped by. We used to do the Gimme Indie Rock radio show on KXCI together in the early 90's, so it was a nice surprise to reconnect with him after so many years.

Also in May, we had our first Airbnb guest from Japan, a nice woman named Yuko. We've had visitors from Europe, Mexico, South America, Africa, India and Pakistan, China but never one from Japan before. When Yuko arrived, we were about to take Dingus for a walk. She asked if she could join us, so together we strolled the streets of Armory Park with its cracked sidewalks under a mesquite canopy.

It was Yuko's third visit to Tucson, but her first time using Airbnb. With her limited English and our non-existent Japanese, we still managed some small talk. She told us she was in town to visit an artist friend. She came from a small village north of Tokyo and her husband didn't enjoy traveling as much as she did. As she checked out, she left us with a couple of packs of Japanese travel wet wipes and candy.

I used to wonder about Fukuoka back when I worked for American Airlines. When a customer would call up to check prices, I'd pull up the city pair, say HEL to FUK and I was like 'what in the hell..?!?' Now, I have a much better idea. I haven't been to Helsinki yet, but I can now say I've been to Fukuoka.

We flew into Tokyo's Haneda airport, arriving at 4 am. Since we were traveling standby, we felt lucky to get out of Tucson, let alone to Japan, as we got the last seats on super full flights from home, then from PHX and finally after a six- hour wait, LAX. We were tired, especially from that last eleven-hour flight across the Pacific, and we were hoping to catch an early JAL flight to Fukuoka, as they ran them practically every hour. Turns out the first flight with any standby seats for airline employees was at 12 pm, so we got to see plenty of the airport, which had a multitude of food options from fresh asparagus and baked goods to neatly packed sweets of all kinds.

After a decent leisurely American breakfast and more exploring of the airport, we headed to our gate. That flight was delayed an hour, but to our surprise, they handed out 1000 yen food vouchers to every passenger. So thanks to JAL, our free lunch was delicious, including hot dogs with avocado sauce and fruit drinks. When we finally got on board, we were amazed at the flight attendants' cheerful attention to detail and teamwork while serving up beverages. I've never seen that with American Airline employees, who seem too stressed out and bitter towards the concept of customer service.

Overall, I was very impressed with how courteous Japanese culture is compared to the states. People here respect each other's space. No such thing as road rage or even honking car horns. Public spaces are kept clean and spotless and most public bathrooms come equipped with warm water bidets as standard equipment.

We landed in FUK, exchanged some currency, and rented a mobile wi-fi device, which I was sure we'd need in future days for navigation here.

We got a taxi to our hotel (much cheaper than Ubers here) and crashed out for a much needed twelve hours of sleep. The hotel breakfast was spectacular with so many choices--miso soup, salmon, kimchi, dumplings plus the bibimbap, omelette, ramen, sushi and waffle stations, just to name a few. I'm discovering my Hilton gig is really paying off in more ways than one. Not only are we saving money on lodging, but our stay usually includes a half off discount on meals at the hotel property plus a complimentary daily and massive breakfast. Especially outside the states, the breakfast buffet will fill you up for most of the day. From our Fukuoka hotel, we walked down the street to check out a shopping mall, which did not resemble the American equivalent at all. Instead of processed fast food, they had fresh seafood, baked goods, fruit and vegetables along with the more typical clothing outlets you find in shopping malls.

I was looking forward to seeing my old friends in Raw Power tonight at the Public Space Yojigen. They had a mini-tour of Japan lined up, starting in Osaka, then Fukuoka, Nagoya, Tokyo and Yokohama. Because we'd failed in earlier attempts to attend their recent gigs in Mexico and Portugal, I didn't even bother telling them we were coming, just in case the non-rev game didn't pan out. From the hotel, I sent Mauro a note on Messenger asking if he could put us on the guest list and he was shocked we were in the country.

We showed up at the cigarette smoke-filled "club" downtown, a room packed like a sardine can. No one spoke practically any English, but eventually I ran into Mauro and the guys and introduced them to Sara. We had brought a few books and t-shirts with us, but for this venue it was impossible to put anything on display. There just wasn't any space for it. The small room, up two flights of stairs, was overflowing with enthusiastic locals, with a few French, Germans and Poles thrown in for good measure.

Trying to make my way up to the bar for a drink was challenging in the tight space. When I succeeded, I was struggling with my pocketful of coins to determine if I had enough to pay for two Camparis. A burly, older Japanese punk gentleman in a black leather jacket slid the coins back towards me on the bar and ordered three of the drinks, took one himself and paid the bartender. A few minutes later, he did the same with another round when Mauro joined us for a toast and a round of sake. No English necessary here.

Raw Power played their hearts out like a well-oiled machine, rumbling out of the gate, building momentum and churning with intensity as one song flowed into another. Their new drummer was a beast, extending a challenge to the older band members to keep up with him. The opening bands were impressive, Step Lightly with their psychedelic dub thrash and heavy hitters AFLS. Live music was alive and well in Fukuoka!

The next day, we took our first bullet train north, getting off in Hiroshima. Stowing our luggage in a locker, we took a bus to the Atomic Dome, the epicenter of the nuclear bomb blast that took place eighty years ago. I had seen photos of this very site ever since I was a child, but actually standing in front of it was something else altogether.

This city was a living hell in 1945. If you survived the blast, the hell only continued. The Hiroshima atomic bombing resulted in an estimated 140,000 deaths by the end of the year. While many died immediately from the blast and heat, the long-term effects of radiation led to more deaths from diseases like leukemia and cancer. What really brought it home was walking through the Hiroshima Peace Memorial Museum, along with dozens of Japanese school children, looking at the displays and horrific photographs of death and burn victims. One display they had was a child's burnt tricycle and helmet and another was a school lunch box and water bottle, with its contents that were never consumed. Today's A bombs are 2000 times more deadly.

Another bullet train took us to Nagoya. Bullet trains have been running here for sixty years, connecting all the major cities and are as efficient as hell. C'mon America, let's try to catch up!

I had last visited Nagoya on a solo trip I took back in the year 2000 that included a visit to Base Record Shop, which has since moved to Tokyo. This time I was here for a show at Huck Finn, the renowned punk club that opened in 1981, the same year that Raw Power got their start. This was a bigger, better organized club than the one in Fukuoka, with a separate room for selling merchandise. The band Ananas, who had supported a similar tour with Raw Power here in 2018, along with the band Jasons opened up. (The bands in Japan are great. Top musicianship and originality are important here and it shows, I discovered.)

That night I also got to meet Andy Murmur who was as excited to meet me as I was to see him. Many years ago, I had heard from former bandmate Angie Garcia that his band Murmur had covered a Peace Corpse song and released it on a flexi-disc, which I found unbelievably flattering as we had broken up decades ago. Andy brought his original copies of the Quincy and Wop Hour 7"s and was ecstatic to get them signed. His bandmates also bought my book and t-shirts, as did a few other locals tonight. In spite of the language barrier, punk rock had brought us together here at a Raw Power gig. As we left in search of a taxi, we felt a true kinship and mutual respect for each other.

The next day, we headed to Tokyo on our final bullet train, zipping through the rural landscape into the gleaming urban center of the world's most populated city where inhabitants number over 37 million. Navigating the immense train system was a mind-boggling adventure. We stashed our baggage in a train station locker. Then we realized we left our pocket wi-fi device inside just as we were about to board a local train and had to go back and retrieve it. After spending hours wandering underneath Tokyo Station, we eventually caught the correct commuter and found the Godzilla store in Shinjuku, only to be dismayed to learn it was just a tiny corner of a huge retail complex. After all the trouble to get to it, we felt obligated to pick up a couple of souvenirs. We went back to Tokyo Station to grab our bags and headed over to Koiwa district for Raw Power's show at the Bush Bash club.

We met Squid here, whom I had just connected with on Instagram the month before. He had flown in from Okinawa to attend his first concert in sixteen years. Squid was taller than your average Japanese man, a quiet, yet friendly music enthusiast who had lived many years in the States. He hosts a podcast called Caffeine Overdose. He bought a copy of the book from me. There were a couple of Italian skinheads who were living in Tokyo chatting up the band as they waited to hit the stage. It was another excellent Raw Power gig, closing out their set with No Way by the Adolescents, Black Flag's White Minority, and the crowd pleaser, Ace of Spades by Motorhead. For me, their original Feed them Grazioli was extra special. It took me back to the fun time I had with them back in 1998 on the Reptile House tour of the U.S.. Here in Tokyo the opening bands Rocky the Sweden and Extinct Government added some excellent local flavor.

We sold a couple more books and shirts before saying goodbye to Mauro, who gave each of us a hug and asked Sara to make sure she keeps me headed in the right direction. We made it to the Tokyo suburb of Ota City for our spartan Airbnb, but not before running into a few happy Raw Power fans at the station and on the subway, two of whom had bought my book from me. Sayonara Tokyo!

I had noticed on social media that a reunion show was announced in Pomona for the band Justice League. They were playing a gig on June 26th a block from our old Toxic Shock location on Locust street. To my

Montreal, QB - Dinner for Sonik Records 40th
Fukuoka, Japan with Mauro of Raw Power
Nagoya City, Japan - with Murmur

Tokyo, Japan - Subway ride

Quebec City - Senior on scooter

Pomona, CA - Farrell of Decry

surprise, evidently in an act of homage, the online flyer read "Toxic Shock Presents". (A couple of Justice League members had actually worked at the Pomona store back in 1986).

I was going to attend a wedding for my nephew Adam in the not too distant high desert town of Hesperia the day after, so I hit up the band to see if they would mind if I set up a merch table featuring my new U.K. book edition. They said no problem, so we figured it might be a fun experience. Before the show, we dropped into Dr. Strange Records for another one of his weekly live streams where we sold a bunch of the new book and other stuff. Earlier in the afternoon we also explored Route 66 (what's left of it anyway on Foothill Blvd) including the Cucamonga Service Station and the Wig Wam Hotel in San Bernardino. For dinner, we had pre-show shenanigans at Pomona's El Merendero with Matt Estel, Bob Durkee, Brian Schmidt and friends. I felt badly for Matt and his sister Meredith as they lost their brother Greg Estel last December in a tragic shooting in Pomona. Greg was an unforgettable, bigger than life soul who I last saw at the BBQ in 2024.

 The show was held at Characters bar near the old antique mall. Decry, Justice League, and openers Bugout and Warcry were all great to see live. It was awesome to see so many (some vaguely) familiar faces in the crowd. Between the live stream at Dr. Strange and the show at Characters, we managed to sell out a box of books, plus some zines and shirts. Marcus Solomon, a guy I'd fired in the late 80's for being "lackadaisical". came up to me and asked if I was hiring. We laughed a bit and he commented that it was cool for me to put on the show. I explained I really had nothing to do with it and as I did in Japan, I was just crashing the party.

When we got home, the interview we did for Squid's podcast in Okinawa was aired, so it seemed like the new book campaign was going pretty well so far this year.

We set our sights on Europe for our next international adventure. Neil Young announced a string of concert dates with the Chrome Hearts and one was in Berlin. I had been to Germany a few times, but it was Sara's first time and it would be my first visit to Berlin. Through Earth Island, I was put in touch with Dario Adamic, who was to be our connection to arrange a book event there.

American Airlines didn't fly into Berlin, but they did go into Frankfurt and Munich. Fingers crossed, I was hopeful we could land in one of the two. Taking the train across Germany was easy. Searching around western Germany, I got in touch with Joseph Raimond and Florian Schuck, who I knew from the Musical Tragedies record label in Nuremberg. Back in the early 90's they had licensed some of the Toxic Shock bands for CD releases, such as Sloppy Seconds, House of Large Sizes, Hullabaloo and also Skinner box. They asked around some Munich and Nuremberg pubs and record stores to see who might be willing to host a book event but nothing was shaping up. I also checked with Underdog Records in Cologne, but was getting nowhere.

Through Facebook, a woman named Gabi Up asked if she could help. She lived in Bamberg, a Upper Franconian Bavarian village that dates back to the 9th Century and is recognized as a Unesco World Heritage Site. She was determined to find a place in her town that would host us and finally found an art gallery that was receptive. She also found a moderator for the event, Susanne Maack.

Luckily, we were able to land into Munich on standby, which made getting to Bamberg fairly easy. Gabi and her boyfriend Bongo met us at the local Biergarten and we walked up the hills of Bamberg, the Venice of Bavaria. It's known as one of Germany's most beautiful towns and man, they weren't wrong! Over beer, we found out Bongo was a Hullabaloo fan and Gabi was a big admirer of GG Allin. We had pizza near a site of public executions during the witch trials held in Bamberg from 1626 to 1632, before walking up to the charming little pub, Galerie Stephansberg.

Joseph from Musical Tragedies was the only person in attendance that I knew prior to 2025. This intimate space was like being in a living room with new friends, in the midst of a storybook Bavarian village. Since the event wasn't going to be held in a very punk rock venue, or even in front of punk music fans necessarily, I had picked a personal chapter about Julianna that I had written on Valentine's Day, 2012. I am not a huge fan of reading my own material, especially the deeply personal stuff, so I had sent Susanne the intro to Chapter 7 from my book, asking if she could translate it into German and read it to the gathering. After she read it, she then pointed out how lucky I was to have Sara as a new chapter in my life. I answered questions, sold a few books and t-shirts and we made some new friends. It was a special afternoon and a wonderful day with lovely people.

Florian from M.T. Records introduced himself as we started to leave the gallery. He had driven up from Nuremberg but missed the reading. He was with his son, who lives in Bamberg and they walked with us down the hills, stopping at a few highlights along the way, such as the Messerschmidt Cafe (famous for their wings!) Then he gave us the choice of seeing the birthplace of Levi Strauss or perhaps the Nazi historical sites of Nuremberg. Being an avid WWII buff, my answer was obvious.

Florian zipped us onto the Autobahn headed south and pulled over by a placid lake. We parked and walked over to Zeppelin Field. This was the site of the humungous Nazi Party rallies, a large deployment area with an imposing concrete grandstand where Hitler would overlook the masses of fanatics, with tanks and other military armament from the

Wehrmacht. On this warm summer day however, there were just a few bored millennials jogging across the area, as dusk set in the peaceful lakeside setting.

Across from the lake was the Congress hall, the largest preserved Nazi government building, although it remained unfinished. Florian drove us up to it, saying he knew of a secret path to drive inside the giant Colosseum-like structure, but unfortunately it was now blocked by chain-link barriers. The highlight for us was driving by the Nazi-era electrical substation that once powered the huge floodlights of the parade grounds. It was still standing, with the shadows of a removed Nazi eagle above the doorway. Oddly, it sat adjacent to a Burger King drive-thru with signs advertising their "Summer Crunch" menu.

The next day, as we were walking from our hotel to our Berlin bound train, we stopped at a few sidewalk-embedded brass plaques that were placed in front of various doorways. These markings represented where Jews were taken from their homes to the death camps. Each one had been stamped with their names and birthdates, the "deportation" dates, which concentration camps they were shipped to, and of course the date and how they perished.

Taking the train across Germany was a breeze. As in Japan, the ICE trains here make travel super simple and efficient. On our arrival in Berlin, we had our first currywurst, (bratwurst slices smothered in a curry ketchup sauce, a Berlin street food specialty) and looked around the Kaiser Wilhelm Cathedral and the rest of Ku'Damm, the Champs d'Elyse or Rodeo Drive of the city, depending on who you ask. Lars Triesch, an architect friend of Ed Colver who had done remodeling work on Frank Zappa's Hollywood home, took us to a traditional German restaurant where the schnitzel was top-notch but a bit pricey.

The next day, we took a train to visit the Sachsenhausen Concentration Camp outside Berlin, in what was formerly East Germany. Built in 1936, in the quiet village of Oranienburg during the Olympics, this, along with Dachau, became a prototype and testing ground for all the camps, both labor and death. To shield the local populace from the horrors taking place inside the camp, a buffer zone of nice homes were built to house the SS officers.

20,000 were imprisoned here, initially for political undesirables. As time went on, the prisoners included homosexuals, gypsies, the disabled, free masons, Jehovah's Witnesses, Russians, and of course, the Jews. The SS held their training here for future camps. Sadistic madness, surgery without anesthesia, and other forms of extreme cruelty were experimented with, institutionalized, and normalized here.

Before we arrived, we had pre-arranged a walking tour of Berlin, done by Jason Honea, a US expat and former singer of the Bay area punk band Social Unrest. We took the wrong bus and were late arrivals at the meeting point. Jason had the charm of an off-duty drill sergeant or perhaps a grizzled P-35 pilot as he pointed out the history of the area. The tour started out at the Anhalter Bahnhof, the mostly bombed out Berlin train station that was opened in 1880. Behind it was the Hochbunker, built in 1943, that housed 3000 people during air raids. Then off on public transport to the historic Alexanderplatz, a central transportation hub in the heart of the city, where protests were held against the East German regime. Heavily graffitied remnants of the Berlin Wall were here, totally encrusted with nasty, used chewing gum. From there we walked to the Reichstag and Brandenburg Gate. We saw several memorials, one for those killed while trying to climb over the Berlin Wall, plus several devoted to the Holocaust, including one for the homosexuals and another for the Sinti and Roma. (We learned that the word gypsy is strictly verboten in Germany.) It was a hot summer day, and my book signing event was that evening, so we had to cut the tour short, and we ended up missing out on seeing the site of Hitler's suicide bunker.

Berlin was one of the more "formal" book signings I've been part of, complete with a wall of photographs, a table covered with white linen tablecloths and a backdrop of black curtains. It was a dual-author event organized by Dario Adamic of No Plan Records, who was also showcasing his own photo books. We had approached several book and record stores, including the big one, Cortex Records, without much success, but finally arranged a reading at an art gallery called Zeitzone in the Kreuzberg neighborhood. We interviewed each other about our respective books and fielded probing questions from the rapt audience members. Many cool punk rock photos circa 1988-89 from his book were on display. Dario really put the extra effort into making this night a success.

I met Florian Helmchen, who had worked at Bonzen Records and who Toxic Shock had licensed th'Inbred's A Family Affair for Europe back in the '80's, and also Robert from Refuse Records, who started a long running hardcore record label in Poland. We all shared stories and had a few laughs. As fun as it turned out to be, since I was unaccustomed to being the social butterfly, I was quite relieved when it was over. I was looking forward to the Neil Young concert the next day.

Waldbuhne amphitheatre is surrounded by forest and was also built in 1936 for the Olympics, part of a megalomaniac architectural plan to reshape Berlin for a Nazi utopia. With the intent of showing the kinship between ancient Greek and Germanic culture, the entrance to Waldbuhne is flanked by two pairs of reliefs by Adolf Wamper: on the left, representing the "Fatherland", are two male nudes, one with a sword, the other with a spear, and on the right, representing artistic celebration, stand two female nudes, one with a laurel wreath, the

 tlin, Germany - Anhalter Bahnhof with Jason Honea

Berlin's Waldbuhne pretzel vendor

Berlin, Germany - Galerie Zeitgeist

Oranienburg, Germany - Sachsenhausen
concentration-camp

Bamberg, Germany - Galerie Stephansberg with Susanne Maack and Joe Raimond

Bamberg Germany with Gabi Up

Rotterdam NL with Butt Plug Santa

other with a lyre. The arena, the Maifeld field, and the Olympic stadium itself were designed to be used together for large events. The deep amphitheatre was lined with rows upon rows of steep concrete steps that led to the stage. We noticed two things. Evidently, Nazis weren't fans of hand rails and today's Germany still loves a good pretzel.

The theatre opened on August 2, 1936, the day after the opening of the Olympic games, with the première of Eberhard Wolfgang Möller's Frankenburger Würfelspiel. 20,000 people were in attendance and the Reich Labour Service supplied 1,200 extras. The theater was also used for some events of the games, in particular boxing matches. During the Olympics and later, dance and choral movement productions took place there, in addition to operas, during the Olympics and again in 1937 for the celebration of the 700th anniversary of Berlin. Tonight, like the Rolling Stones and Bob Marley have done before, that ancient Nazi history was erased by loud rock and roll with Neil Young and the Chrome Hearts. Stick it up your ass, Adolf!

From Berlin, we boarded another ICE train to Cologne, dropped off our bags at the hotel and took another commuter train to Monchengladbach. Neil Young was playing another gig here and we had tickets.

While on the train coming into town, I got a message from Jeffrey Ladd, another US expat who currently lives in Cologne. He heard of the book tour somehow and asked if I had any Peace Corpse t-shirts with me. I told him we were taking a train to the concert soon, but if he could meet me at the station, I'd bring one with me. Jeffrey met me at the station and I made the sale. Quickest mail-order I've ever filled!

We made it to Monchengladbach for the show. Sparkassen Park, the poster said. Maybe that was German for Spark Plug Park. It was held on a flat asphalt race track, with crummy acoustics, one of the least appealing venues we've been to in some time. In the last year or so, Neil would sometimes comment at different appearances on how lucky the locals were to have such a lovely venue. This was not the case here. At least they had a booth serving up Doner Kebabs, the Turkish version of a gyro. Yum!

The band went through their set. It wasn't terrible by any means, but we enjoyed the performance in Berlin so much more. We cut out during the encore of Rockin in the Free World so we could beat the traffic for the train back to Cologne. Looking back on it, I kinda wish we would have skipped this one and spent more time in Cologne, with its magnificent landmark, the Godzilla of cathedrals, but we had to leave early in the morning for Amsterdam.

It was impossible to find an employee rate at any Amsterdam Hilton, but we did find one for a three-night stay in Rotterdam, an hour away by train. My book event was at Occii, a long-running, volunteer-run and nonprofit club. There was going to be a record fair which I was invited to attend,-from 3 pm to 6 and a big birthday bash for Jos (of the 80's straight-edge skatecore band Larm and currently in Seein' Red) later that night.

To save time, we went directly to Amsterdam with our bags in tow and found Occi. We set up our table at 2 pm and poked around to look at the other vendors' offerings, while we waited for people to show up. My connection in Amsterdam was Marko, from the hardcore band Vitamin X and was, like Dario in Berlin, another Bosnian. I had my publisher Earth Island send Marko a box of books and I'm glad we did, because I sold all I had in Berlin.

A few record geek folks made the scene but it really wasn't too busy. Around 3 pm, a nice but annoying older lady kept wasting our time by asking us to put things on hold while she tried to figure out how to load payment apps on her phone. She did the same with all the other vendors, and as time went on, it was obvious she had no Euros to spend. After an hour of this nonsense and due to our waning energy level, Sara and I decided to cut out. We declined Marko's offer for us to stay for the show, where a much bigger crowd was expected. I wished Jos a happy birthday, bought a vinyl copy of Raw Power's Reptile House and said goodbye to Occi. We were tired from all the recent travel and we still had to find our hotel in Rotterdam.

After resting up, the next day we took the train back to Amsterdam to see the sights. It was a rainy day, but Sara had bought tickets for a Canal Cruise with unlimited wine and cheese, so we couldn't pass that up. Afterwards, we soaked up the sights and more rain as we strolled around the city and found a spaghetti house to dry our bones, before heading back to our hotel in Rotterdam.

We spent Monday afternoon exploring Rotterdam itself, which was far less crowded with tourists than Amsterdam and full of charm on its own. The weather was much nicer too. We found the notorious butt plug gnome-like Santa Claus statue on our way to visit a museum.

During WWII, this city was bombed to smithereens by the Luftwaffe, forcing the Dutch to surrender to Germany. It was occupied by the Nazis from 1940 to 1945. They have a museum devoted to this period, but like everywhere else we wanted to go, like record stores, it was closed on Monday. Damn, Rotterdam! We explored the weird, angular Cube houses, tilted on poles like an abstract treehouse. We also went to the gigantic Markthal.which was like a giant food court inside a huge airplane hanger sized art museum.

Unlike Trump's idea of America, the Netherlands welcomes immigrants and it makes for a better, more diverse population with endless culinary options. I finally found one record store open that day, called Velvet, and talked the owner into trading a couple of Barricaded Suspects LPs for some used records. We flew home from Amsterdam the next morning. Back in Tucson, I did an interview for a podcast called "You Don't Know Mojack" that normally involves spiels from SST Records-related bands and people. We discussed the early days of Toxic Shock Records, the Yippie!/punk connection and some legendary live events, such as when Peace Corpse opened for Black Flag in 1983. Thanks to Brant Palko for the opportunity. It was an honor to be asked.

Before we left for Europe, I had worked on setting up a "Two Authors" book trip, together with Sluggo Cawley, who we last saw earlier in the year at the Grannies last show in San Francisco.. We called it the "Dust Trail Twins" book tour. He's always been a great storyteller and his book, Guitargonaut is chock full of those. We flew into Salt Lake City and met up with Sluggo, who flew in from Portland.. Another Toxic Shock figure from the past, John Shafer, a fan of Hullabaloo who had done our wholesale in Pomona joined us for lunch and then drove us to the legendary Raunch Records. I hadn't seen the owner, Brad Collins since 1986 when Raw Power and the Dayglo Abortions blew through Salt Lake on tour.

Brad's always been a great guy and a pillar in his community, and we go back quite a ways. He surprised us with a pile of collaboration t-shirts, featuring both the Toxic Shock and Raunch original logos drawn by Pushead. On the back of the shirt was the book tour poster that Sluggo had designed. Such a nice, meaningful gesture. Also in attendance was James Shuman "El Cid", the singer of the Massacre Guys. I gave him a Barricaded Suspects LP and he dug up one of his old band shirts to give me.

Sluggo and I had done a local community radio interview a few days prior to this so there were a decent amount of people for this one. We each sold a good amount of books and just generally had a good time. The music was blasting on the stereo, so we didn't feel the need to do a reading.

The next morning, bright and early, at 3 am to be exact, we boarded the eastbound California Zephyr. Sluggo took some great photos with his 35mm camera during the 15-hour journey, as we climbed up, through and down the Rockies. We arrived in Denver on Saturday night.

Sluggo and I got an invitation to stay at Deb Vernet's house. Deb was once a member of the all female grunge/punk band Mudwimmen and a very gracious host. We used her house as a base of operations. A few months back, local promoter Ricardo Alvarado mentioned he could set up a string of book events in Colorado that would include Denver, Boulder, Colorado Springs, and Pueblo. I had secured a date with Wax Trax in Denver for Labor Day which was on a Monday, but we figured we could tackle two cities on Sunday.

We first drove down to Colorado Springs for a quick visit to the Garden of the Gods. It was insanely crowded, being a holiday weekend, but a spectacular place with red sandstone rock formations.

Before the book event, knowing that he lived in the area, we invited Wayne Keeler to lunch. He was one of the first Toxic Ranch employees when we opened our shop in Tucson on Grant Road. He got the job referral from Ian MacKaye. He was the singer of the pop-punk band G Whiz. He was also Julianna's favorite person that worked at the shop. Since those long gone days, he had an extensive career in the Army, serving in Iraq and Afghanistan and climbing the ranks all the way to Major.

We met at the Airplane Restaurant by the Air Force Academy. Sluggo got the Flying Fortress salad, Sara and Wayne got the Afterburner burger, and I ordered the Reuben Von Crashed. While we consumed our food, Wayne entertained us with a few yarns. Afterwards, we headed to the first venue today, What's Left Records and set up our table.

Again the stereo was blasting, and there were very few customers while we were there. Wayne made up for it by doing a reenactment of a Sick of it All video, featuring hardcore dance moves, including "making pizza" and "picking up change". As we wrapped things up, Wayne told me that he thought Julianna would be proud of what I had accomplished with the book. That meant a great deal to me. The record store owner, Byran, bought a few books and records from us, so we bid farewell to him and Keeler and loaded up for our next stop in Pueblo.

We found the Blo Back Gallery and met Ricardo. Turns out today was the last day of the Colorado State Fair, so most of the city's populace was attending that, but a few people showed up and they couldn't have been nicer. We had three opening acts, two poets and a punk rock banjo player. The stage was then set up with two chairs and two microphones. Sluggo and I provided the night's headline entertainment by interviewing each other and taking questions from the folks, ending up with some polite applause. We sold a few books and called it a night, before driving back to Denver.

I've known Duane and Cindy Davis, owners of Wax Trax, for decades now. Like Raunch, they were a regular account when Toxic Shock first became a record distributor in 1982 and remained a regular for many years. They had visited Toxic Ranch in the late'90's when they were in Tucson on vacation.

My first visit to their shop was in November 1984 during a Denver stop on the Peace Corpse/Decry tour. At that time, they also had a shop across the street from the record store that sold t-shirts, called Across the Trax, which Cindy managed. They, along with a handful of others, continued to be supporters of our business over the decades with t-shirt orders which kept us going in the lean summer months. It was great to see them again.

I kept in touch with Duane via Facebook and lately we commented on each other's travel adventures. Whenever I found myself in Denver, I would reach out to see if he'd be at the shop, to no avail. Finally, while looking at cities to hold book signings for the Dust Trail Twins, I was able to confirm a date with Delaney, one of the current managers at Wax Trax. She put me in touch with the local community radio station KGNU to help promote it. I asked her if she thought Duane would be willing to be the moderator for the Labor Day event. Duane and Cindy had basically retired from the store, but to my delight, Duane emailed me back to confirm.

Sara and I arrived early and we perused the record bins while the Wax Trax crew set up our table and a couple of microphones. Sluggo and his wife, Laurian, showed up with some of their friends. We arranged our table display and then Duane and Cindy dropped in. We exchanged our salutations and shortly after, Duane pulled out a list of questions from his pocket and picked up a microphone.

Sluggo had a good amount of his friends in attendance and there were a couple of Tucson people there as well. With moderator extraordinaire Duane guiding us along, we did our spiel along with some banter and had a really fun time. Both Sluggo and I sold a bunch of stuff and did some bartering with the Wax Trax crew to try and empty ourselves of our wares. As we wrapped things up, Duane asked me where our next stop on the book tour would be. For once, I didn't have an answer. Usually I had my book tour arranged two months in advance but now I was looking forward to spending time at home as the worst of Tucson's summer heat was winding down.

We had arranged today's book event in the afternoon, to allow us enough time to catch, you guessed it, another Neil Young concert, this one at Fiddler's Green Amphitheatre. Since we had a super early flight home the next morning, we swung by Deb's house to say our farewells. The night's show was filled with seventeen songs including Cowgirl in the Sand, Sun Green, and the debut, for us anyway, of a new song called Big Crime, a scathing indictment of a song directed at the current administration.

During the course of the book tour and the time that led up to it, I've learned a valuable lesson of the importance of maintaining contact with friends and meeting new people on this journey called life. Our time on this planet is indeed finite and life should be experienced and enjoyed to the best of one's ability. Sure, you can procrastinate, but from my perspective, experiences are more important than owning objects or stashing money away for a rainy day. As a wise man once said, "It's better to regret something you have done than to regret something that you haven't done". Like Edith Piaf, "Je ne regrette rien."

Salt Lake City, Utah with Sluggo and
Brad at Raunch Records
Denver, CO getting sage advice from
Duane at Wax Trax Records
Travel by Train!
Tucson, AZ lunch at La Indita
with Janet Brown

Phoenix AZ

Bombay Beach CA

Minnesota State Fair

Atomic Dome Hiroshima Japan

Tucson AZ

Glenwood Springs CO

Niagara Falls Canada

Santa Barbara CA

Route 66 San Bernardino CA

Meat Puppets Phoenix AZ
Flipper with Mike Watt Ventura CA
Os Mutantes at Meow Wolf in Santa Fe NM

TV Smith of the Adverts in San Diego
Crazy Horse in Nashville TN
Ween in Spokane WA
Neil Young solo Los Angeles CA

Grannies last show San Francisco

the Beaumonts at Corn Lovers Fiesta Austin TX

Raw Power in Toyko Japan

TOXIC SHOCK
RECORDS
ASSASSIN OF MEDIOCRITY
A STORY OF LOVE, LOSS AND LOUD MUSIC
by BILL SASSENBERGER
TOXIC SHOCK
ASSASSIN OF MEDIOCRITY
RECORDS T-SHIRTS VIDEO
379   GIFTS 622-5641
RAW POWER
DECRY
HICKOIDS
KENT STATE
ZERO BOYS
SLOPPY SECONDS
EARTH ISLAND BOOKS

TOXIC SHOCK RECORDS
by Bill Sassenberger

Book release and signing!

"Toxic Shock is a full color, 204-page book that chronicles the history of the punk record store/mail order enterprise and groundbreaking record label Toxic Shock from its origins in 1980 in the grimy suburbs of Pomona, CA to its demise in Tucson, AZ in 2014."

DJ set by Shane Muldowney & guests!

April 20th, 6-8 PM
Wooden Tooth Records
108 E. Congress St

BLO BACK GALLERY PRESENTS:
DUST TRAIL TWINS
BILL SASSENBERGER & SLUGGO CAWLEY
READING FROM THEIR BOOKS ON PUNK ROCK

WITH SPECIAL GUESTS
EL BANJO BONES
SCOOT
GEORGE BATUELLO

SUNDAY // AUGUST 31, 2025 // 5PM

BLO BACK GALLERY-131 SPRING STREET-PUEBLO CO-81003
PHOTO BY RAYMOND RIHNER
EARTH ISLAND BOOKS

TOXIC SHOCK RECORDS: ASSASSIN OF MEDIOCRITY
BOOK READING & SIGNING WITH BILL SASSENBERGER

SATURDAY, JUNE 22
2PM AT AMOEBA BERKELEY

Reading is free, MUST purchase Toxic Shock at Amoeba Berkeley to attend signing.

FRIDAY, JUNE 7
AN IN-STORE APPEARANCE + BOOK SIGNING WITH
BILL SASSENBERGER

COME MEET BILL SASSENBERGER OF TOXIC SHOCK RECORDS! HEAR STORIES ABOUT ONE OF THE MOST LEGENDARY & INFLUENTIAL CALIFORNIA PUNK ROCK STORES AND RECORD LABELS OF ALL TIME!

2-4PM
at Dr. Strange RECORDS
7136 Amethyst Ave, Alta Loma, CA 91701

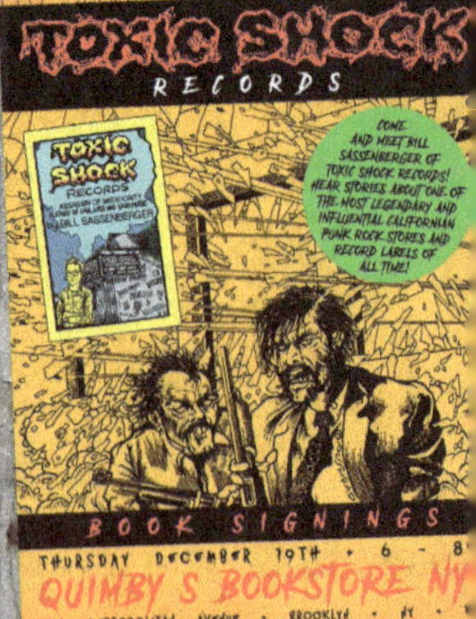